UNSTOPPABLE!

25 inspirational stories from women
in business who overcame adversity
to create a powerful legacy

The Queenie Effect Publishing

Copyright © 2023 The Queenie Effect Publishing

Foreword by Shamina Taylor

All rights reserved. No part of this publication may be reproduced, stored in a retrieval system, or transmitted in any form or by any means, electronic, mechanical, photocopying, recording or otherwise, without the prior written permission from both the copyright owner and publisher.

Disclaimer

All the information, techniques, skills, and concepts contained within this publication are of the nature of general comment only and are not in any way recommended as individual advice. The intent is to offer a variety of information to provide a wider range of choices now and in the future, recognising that we all have widely diverse circumstances and viewpoints. Should any reader choose to make use of the information contained herein, this is their decision and the author and publishers do not assume any responsibilities whatsoever under any condition or circumstances.

Foreword by Shamina Taylor

It is a great honor and privilege to be able to write the forward for this incredible book Unstoppable.

Elsa is a true natural-born leader. This woman is the epitome of strength, courage, and determination. She is a woman who is leaving a legacy along with the other women in Unstoppable.

I am so grateful that I have personally mentored Elsa and several other authors in this book. Elsa is THE definition of unstoppable. There is nothing this woman will let stand in her way from what she knows is possible and her attaining it. She is a humble hustler and destined for immeasurable greatness.

There are very few women who can measure up to her ability to keep going even when there are no guarantees things are working out. Her faith in herself and her mission is commendable. She is a woman who will never give up. To say she is inspiring is an understatement. She has faced every struggle you can think of in this lifetime and Elsa is the poster woman for the saying, "Get knocked down 7 times, get up 8'. That is Elsa. She has overcome one setback after another just to turn them into stepping into a stepping stones on her journey to success.

What does it mean to be unstoppable?

I believe it is when nothing is going to slow us down or stop us for long in the pursuit of what we want to achieve in our lives and business. It is an energy only the 1% possess. You know, the extraordinary ones we see as unicorns.

Being unstoppable, is knowing no failure, setback, thought, belief, circumstances are going to get in the way of you accomplishing what you came here to do.

To be unstoppable requires you to face truths about yourself you might not have before. As we are the ones who are the only way standing in the way of our successes.

Not everyone is wired to be unstoppable, BUT I do believe everyone has the opportunity to become unstoppable if they are able to harness the power of their mindset to go all in on their vision no matter what.

As you read through the stories from every woman in this book, you will see each one was faced with incredible challenges throughout their life, but that did not stop her. She overcame them again and again, hence they embodied what it means to be unstoppable.

Along with Elsa, there are few other women in this book I have personally mentored sharing their stories, and I have watched several of these women transform their lives into becoming the most powerful version of themselves in a very short period of time.

These women have dug deep and done the inner work many will not do to find what they are truly made of. You will feel the magic of their stories and the success they each were able to achieve.

The women you will read about have faced failures, lacked confidence, lacked belief in themselves, had moments in their lives that came with extreme struggles. You will see how each displayed an act of resilience, never giving up on themselves or their vision and the impact they came here to make.

Get a pen and some kleenex, as you read the stories, you will shed tears as they will resonate deeply, and the wisdom these women shared will have you taking notes so you can implement some of their knowledge. You may also have some clarity and gain an understanding on understanding on maybe why you haven't been able to get to that next level of success, and maybe now have a road map to help you get that unstoppable momentum going.

If you really want to release yourself from the chains of inaction, remove the barriers and resistance to why you haven't gone all- in yet on your dreams, READ unstoppable with an open mind, and allow yourself to receive all the magic throughout this book. It will change your life and help you find that fire in you to start taking action in your life and business.

After reading this book, you just might find a new belief in yourself that you've known was deep in, just waiting to be awakened.

Ready to be motivated and inspired to become unstoppable?

Then this book is for you.

Shamina Taylor
Wealth Expert, Business Menor, and Attorney

Shamina Taylor, Attorney turned Wealth Expert and Mentor, helps high-achieving women level up in their personal lives and in their businesses by teaching them how to become the most powerful, fulfilled, wealthy, and successful version of themselves.

With over 20 years of experience, Shamina is a top industry leader and has helped hundreds of women build their businesses, both on- and offline. Her top clients are making up to 100k a month in recurring revenue and have multiple 7 figure businesses. Shamina herself has had a record-breaking year. Her business crossed the 7-figure cash received mark in less than ten months. She's also a recipient of the 2021 Two Comma Club Award for earning over one million with ClickFunnels.

Shamina is the Host of The Quantum Woman Podcast and has spoken at Unfair Advantage Life, The Intuitive Entrepreneur, and The Smarter Income Stream. She is also the creator of numerous online programs, including Infinite Wealth, Accessing the Quantum, Magnetic Power, and a high-caliber Mastermind designed to move women to their next level fast. With a combined social media following of over 50k, Shamina has been featured on Washington DC's ABC7, CBS's Virginia This Morning, ABC Sacramento's Your California Life, Medium's Authority Magazine, and Thrive Global.

Introduction

This book is the culmination of many years of work. Bringing together powerful women who share their stories of overcome, lack of belief, sadness, and heartbreak... to where they are today.

Unstoppable women who could have been stopped, but they weren't.

Women who could have stayed where they were, but they chose to keep going.

Women who got back up again for their families, their children and, more importantly, for themselves.

This is the beginning of a beautiful relationship between story-telling & impact. This is the magic between adversity and hope. This is the creation of generational curses being broken, movements of change and ever-lasting impact.

These women came together, unified to impact thousands and thousands of women. They committed to the evolution of change, the disruption within their cocoon, and the butterfly's emergence. Some share their stories for the very first time, and others to affirm they are on the right path.

Unstoppable is a message of hope, transformation, inspiration, motivation, education and love. It shows you what you can achieve when you cannot be stopped and what can happen when you keep going.

This book will create a movement for women and be the lighthouse to show them the way. It is the GPS. The compass. The roadmap.

I dedicate this book to my family: my husband Olaf, my two children Alfie and Georgie, my parents Alfirio & Celina and my brother Victor. Without them, I would not be here. This is my Legacy for you.

To the authors of this book, I thank you for your contribution, and I know this is the beginning of where you spread your wings and fly. Thank you for being so transparent, loving, and REAL in your mission to serve.

To my coaching clients, I am humbled to play a part in your journey and thank you for gifting me the opportunity to be a part of your transformation to greatness.

To my mentors who helped shape who I am, I am indebted to the insight, knowledge and expertise you shared so I can grow and expand.

And lastly, to my 9-year-old self…. Thank you for holding the fort. Thank you for being as strong as you were and reminding me how much stronger I can be. You did good. I got this now.

Elsa Morgan
CEO & FOUNDER, The Queenie Effect PTY LTD

Contents

Elsa Morgan 1

Agi Mooy 17

Andrea Stevens 33

Bonnie Clark Harris 47

Bwalya Desmond 61

Christine McFarlane-Olsen 73

Deneen Iverson-Kidd 87

Denny Hunt 95

Geraldine Schollum 109

Jane S Tennis 125

Janet Schoen 137

Kate Trevean 151

Kellie Zentz 165

Leanne Makinson 177

Lisa Dias 191

Lyndee Nicholson 205

Maria Douglas 219

Marlo Fullerton 235

Melissa Sutherland 249

Rachael Hall 263

Susan Kommor 273

Suz Tutty 291

Terri-Lynn Chaplin 305

Theresa Seitz 319

Valerie Thurman 333

Elsa Morgan

The power of the word…. YET

"Do you know who you are speaking to?" I asked into the phone. "I mean… this is me, Elsa Morgan. You must be mistaken."

And she repeated….

"You are going to impact thousands of women.
You will create coaching programs
You will speak on stages around the world, training & impacting thousands of women around the globe"

That's what my healer, Helen Fernandez, said. I remember looking at my phone, confused. "Ummm, okay. But I am not at seven figures," I responded.

"Yet…." She replied.

Yet. One of the most powerful words in the dictionary.

Unstoppable!

It was that word, yet, that had me hope and dream that her words rang true.

When she spoke those words, I was living back with my parents, my husband and our two children in one bedroom. It was purely out of necessity because we moved back from our investment property in Noosaville to be with family, my parents, in Melbourne.

I didn't know it then, but that fateful conversation on that day would ring true one day. I just did not see it back in 2020. Yet.

My life can best be described as being the tale of the underdog.

Underestimated. Misunderstood. Misinterpreted. The great thing is most people who do anything significant in life are described this way.

I was born poor. I had two dining chairs as my bed for the first 18 months of my life. That would soon change.

My native country, Argentina, is where my father decided one day to immigrate to Australia. His family called him crazy. He did not know the English language, no understanding of the Australian culture and no family. Yet, one thing my father never lacks is courage.

And this is one of many traits he has taught me about life. About me.

Growing up, I was someone who was constantly pursuing goals. My father taught me that too. Best to go "ALL IN" or don't go there at all.

This drive and determination have given me the energy and focus to achieve goals. Even though I received relatively good grades in school, I consider myself street-smart more so than booksmart. I go by feel and "gut". This is what has propelled me more than anything else.

I never saw myself as a "winner" naturally. I knew I 'could' win if I had just started and went all in.

Once I was in school, my parents moved around until we finally settled at Charlbury Grove in St.Albans. This is where I lived throughout my teenage years, and would shape me into the woman I became. By the time we moved there, I had already been in two different primary schools and would eventually have attended four different primary schools by the time I finished.

I was brought up in a strict environment, and it never occurred to me how fortunate I am. I was brought up in an environment with strong values, and yet I realise now how much this also shaped me into the woman I have become.

Nothing was ever given to us. We had to earn our way. We made our beds from a young age, and I helped mum as much as possible in the kitchen after school.

My parents both worked in the factory, oftentimes 12-hour shifts. Mum would wake me up at 5 am and take me to the lounge with my blanket and pillow. She would turn on the TV and switch it to "Rocky & Bullwinkle". My school clothes were ready, my lunch packed, and this was my routine through my forming years.

I knew back then that I was not going to work 12-hour shifts. I just knew it wasn't for me. After high school, I was accepted to study Bachelor of Business Marketing/Economics at Victoria University. It was not until my fourth & final year, with four subjects to go, that I decided it was not for me. I had already been working in the Marketing department at a large company in my 3rd year of University and realised that it was not what I wanted to do.

And this very much reflected my life in my 20s. I had several jobs ranging from Telesales to Business Development. I was really good in my roles, but I often became dissatisfied after achieving the goals. It was no longer a challenge. Looking back, I could see that my programming of having to hit goals to feel worthy

I didn't know it then, but this programming is what would potentially hold me back. Once I finally did realise this, I had already filed for bankruptcy, had maxed out credit cards and had been divorced by my mid-30s.

My bankruptcy was a blessing in disguise.

I remember how bad I felt when I told my parents about my decision. I felt like a failure. My parents, who gave up all for myself and my brother to provide us with a better life… and here I was telling them how badly I had screwed up. Even though the shame around admitting that "you got it wrong" ate me up inside, I knew that it was a road I had to travel alone.

"Make the decision… but make sure you learn the lesson," my father said.

Single, Bankrupt and having no idea what life had installed for me. These words would haunt me for a long time as I began a new chapter of being on my own and learning how to live paycheck to paycheck. It was not long after that I decided to move to Brisbane to start my new life. During the next 3.5 years, I lived with good friends, lived on my own and started to understand more about what I wanted in life. I was starting the healing process. Up until then, I never really had a voice. I always went along with what everyone else wanted me to do. But it was during this time that I started to figure out that I was destined for me, and I could do big things if I tapped into my courage and bravery more.

I joined a running club and fell in love with the community. Running was my constant, my best friend and the only time I could "think" When I ran, I would think about my life, all the events that lead me to that day, trying to understand or make meaning of it. Running made me feel good about myself and it made me feel okay. I bumbled my way through life until 2012, when Life started to change, fast.

One day in early 2012, after work, I got a call from my mother. It was Dad. He had been diagnosed with prostate cancer. This gave me the biggest shock. My father, the strong, hard-working man who I knew, was suddenly affected by this disease. Luckily I worked for the airline, which allowed me to jump on a plane on a Friday and see my parents. This was just what I needed, a bolt in the system. I had already decided that at the end of 2012, I would pack up and go home because I knew my family needed me.

Of course, as always, after that decision, my world was shocked when I met a handsome Englishman online. We had many long and exciting conversations before we decided it was time to meet. Needless to say, I was totally in awe of his handsome looks. He was (and still is) intelligent, clever, witty, and everything I could ever hope for in someone I could share my life with. I remember one day, he seemed distracted, and I asked him what was on his mind. He admitted that he was unsure because he knew I was moving to Melbourne. He didn't want to get hurt. "What is stopping you from coming with me?" I asked. He sat with that for a bit and said..... "nothing".

And thus began my next chapter, with my soulmate and best friend, now husband.. Olaf. We packed up our life and drove in my trusty grey Toyota Yaris to Melbourne to start our new life together at the end of 2012.

Together we travelled everywhere, including Nepal, Thailand, and the UK, and we continued to run distant races, including half-marathons and marathons.

Fast-forward to 2015, we were living in Coburg when we welcomed our first child, Alfie. I was so in love. Handsome, with beautiful eyes... I knew he would change my life. And yet I was not feeling right. I was going through post-natal depression, and it was a challenge. What was more challenging was losing my baby weight. I was always slim because I ran and trained for running races. I naively thought my weight would drop down instantly after Alfie was born. How wrong was I? I could not shake it off. During May, I remember seeing my friend post about a product she took and how amazing it was. I had previously seen her post about it on social media, yet I was sceptical. And this was a friend I trusted. But on this day, I decided to give this product a go, fully expecting it to not work.

I was wrong. I lost all the weight... so did Olaf, who joined to keep me accountable.

I felt amazing, fitting back into my clothes and people began asking me how I had lost all the weight. I reached out to my friend and asked her how my friends could access the same products. She showed me my link and casually mentioned that I would earn a $200 bonus for every system I sold.

Hang on.. what? Little did she know then. But I had been looking for an alternative career that would allow me to stay home. THIS WAS IT! She then sent me a video showcasing people earning income and staying home with their families whilst building their businesses.

And so began the next chapter of our lives... we entered the world of network marketing.

Little did I know what exactly was involved, but the lessons I learned in the first 2.5 years would serve me as the years continued.

Along the way, there were many days that I felt I was in control of building the business but had lost touch with household duties or spending time with my family. Or even worse, no downtime for me. Or, I would go out to family gatherings and needed to learn how to manage my time.

I struggled to enrol the people I wanted to work with. I was attracting people that had different values than me, yet I honestly had no idea where I was going wrong.

Fast-forward to one fateful day when I called on a friend who had been in home businesses for over 20 years to ask for his advice. I explained exactly what I was experiencing. I was sending out messages and posting on social media; yet, I had one person building the business and only a few customers. "Do you have a coach or mentor whom you follow?" He asked. I admitted that I did, but I did not do everything he had advised me to do. "Well, there is your problem he said. You need to follow a blueprint, a system, a process". And there it was. That was precisely what I was NOT doing. I was not following the proven method.

From that day, I decided to commit to listening to my coach and mentors and implement everything they taught me to do to build a business every single day, no matter what.

Since that day in late 2017, I have committed to showing up

every day and building my business online. Not only did I do all the things I was taught, but I also started to see results. Consistently.

It was through showing up consistently that I learned about how important it was to have a system to be able to treat your business like a business. I started strengthening my mindset and learned the 'proper way' to market myself on social media to attract the right people into my business.

I did find, though, that nothing worked more than building the consistency muscle and showing up every single day, regardless of what was happening in my life and business. This truly was the biggest learning from my coach. The art of showing up when all was well, when it was hard, and especially when nobody was watching.

After a few years in the profession and having achieved much success, I discovered that I had a gift of being able to relate to women over 40. After all, I was 40-something too. Like them, I had "life experience", I had a family, I had commitments, baggage and had experienced many of the challenges that they were experiencing.

I had earned trips, hit the top of compensation plans, earned car bonuses. I knew how to achieve success. It was time for me to show others how.

I toyed with the idea of launching my coaching program. Eeeeh…. My program. I was scared as hell, but then I thought, 'If not me, then who? If not now, then when?"

I remember Helen's words and how I would have my program. And here I was.

I remember thinking to myself…. I knew I could do this. After all, I had helped many women develop online businesses generating their first 3-figure, 4-figure, and 5-figure monthly cheques. I had helped women achieve 6-figure incomes online (disclaimer, this all required a blueprint that was followed, and they did the work).

I knew that there was an opportunity to fulfil my vision of helping over 100,000 women directly and indirectly, contributing $25,000 cheques every month to charity.

I started to map out my programs based on my systems. These were systems I had created and made my own. These were processes that I had developed that helped me to generate the successes that I had achieved and continue to achieve to this day.

A good friend recommended I partner with a company that successfully launched new coaches, and I again invested in a coach. This was over $5000, and I knew it was "game time".

Again, I followed the blueprint my coach advised me to do. I did everything that he suggested.

In May 2021, I launched my coaching business, and since then, we have helped hundreds of women achieve their goals with my proven 3-step system. The foundation of my programs is to help women understand that they can build their businesses online around their family, work, and commitments. I am determined to help them get organised, follow a proven system, become consistent and show up every day in their business whilst balancing the demands in their lives.

We have also created events and provided speaking opportunities, and I am now publishing my first book, showcasing many of my incredible coaching clients.

It's been an enormous success. Over 80 percent of my clients have achieved the best months, been promoted in their work, or started service-based businesses. And I am just getting started.

For example, one of my clients, B, not only started attracting new customers after just one coaching call with me but earned herself bonuses from her company, extra SWAG, and prizes. From the very beginning of our partnership, we set up her schedule and worked together with the system I used to build my business every day. She managed to block out time in her calendar, to work her business around her full-time job and family commitments whilst still achieving results. She has also earned her first 5-figure month.. and then went ahead and did it again.

True story, she had already regained one-quarter of the investment from my one-on-one coaching program after two coaching calls.

My systems work, and I continuously strive to bring the best out of myself for my clients.

My company is scaling to 7 figures as we speak, and my online business has grown over 300 per cent. I am fortunate, yet I know that my street smart and grit have gotten me here.

I get asked how I achieved all the things I did. Three things I know that have accelerated my growth:
1. You are the average of the five people you spend the most time with. This is true in life as it is in business
2. Success is the sum of small, actionable steps taken every day
3. If you want to change your life, raise your standards.

Who would have thought that a woman, born into poverty with two dining chairs as her bed for the first 18 months of her life could do this?

Me. I never gave up on myself.

Every single day I wake up and back Me.

Deep down inside, I knew that to create the movement, the change, and the impact I wanted to create, I must first believe that I could do it. And whilst on many occasions I have had to borrow my mentors belief in me, I never stopped believing that I was meant for more.

Impacting 100,000 women might sound BIG, HAIRY & AUDACIOUS, but it starts with one woman first.

It may as well be me.

About the Author

Elsa Morgan is a 49-year-old founder & CEO of The Queenie Effect, a company whose mission is to impact over 100,000 women and contribute $25,000 cheques to charities every month. Through her programs, Elsa has impacted hundreds of women's lives. She is a best-selling author and has been featured in the New Journal & Entrepreneurs Herald.

Her business is currently scaling to 7 figures and has an online business that has grown exponentially. She is an avid real estate investor and, together with her husband, manages a multi-million dollar investment portfolio.

She has over 20 years of Sales & Marketing experience, having generated over $100 million in signed contracts during that time. She is wife to her best friend and business partner, Olaf and mother to two beautiful children.

Facebook: www.facebook.com/elsabmorgan
Instagram: www.instagram.com/therealelsamorgan/

Agi Mooy

Chosen

In my mind, sitting at my engagement dinner in a gorgeous fuchsia crepe dress, blonde hair flowing, eyes intently on my Husband- to- be and sipping champagne. I wasn't yet 21 years old, proud of being a Mum to my handsome two-year-old boy Josh, not thinking about the impact on his life due to my decision to divorce his father.

The feeling of being free at that time outweighed future thoughts.

My Life was blessed, charmed and exciting. Looking back over the last 40+ years, joining the dots, I can honestly say I was 'chosen' for each assignment, and clearly, God had plenty of those for me.

Chosen. Chosen to show my Family, Friends, and significant others, that the option of 'getting back up' is far less painful than staying down.

The question I get asked daily by people I speak to now is,

'how many times do you get knocked down before you give up?'

As I go back even further in my mind, I now recognise that asking for help was a huge block, so difficult. Was it an inbuilt generational sign of weakness?

My Father was a Holocaust and Concentration Camp Survivor. With that trauma and ordeal, asking for help was not an option. Since my dad's passing, I have visited Auschwitz and seen the hopelessness with my own eyes.

Viktor E. Frankl was an Austrian psychiatrist and neurologist who survived the Holocaust through four concentration camps, including the notorious Auschwitz. His experiences in these camps inspired him to develop a unique form of psychotherapy that had, at its core, the belief that if you can't change a situation, you should change the way you look at that situation.

"When we are no longer able to change a situation, we are challenged to change ourselves.

It's the secret to removing the blocks that cause you to see situations negatively so that you can be happier and more successful in your life, business and relationships.

Reinventing myself began as a fairy tale. I was surrounded by the rich and famous lifestyle, rubbing shoulders with the

Movie Stars of the 80s due to the position my new Husband, Evan, held in the Movie Industry. How exciting! My job in the finance and service industry was fun too. I worked up through the ranks from teller to loans officer to manager in a busy City branch. Life was perfect, and with a busy, crazy, yet completely fulfilled life comes baby Boy number 2, Bradley.

Life was perfect. We had lots of conversations and were getting to know some soccer families through my son Josh. We had a proposal laid out from a couple we became good friends with. It required moving to the Country and taking on a run-down Hotel to build it back up. Interesting challenge…and we both agreed let's make this tree change for the Boys. I then needed to upskill and study for my liquor license. Once that was complete, the move began to the Country.

Looking back, I had terrible push and pull going on, so much broken heart leaving my Father behind and yet wanting the best for the Boys. Leaving my Father was so hard on us all. He didn't want to come with us, as my Brother had unexpectedly passed away three years earlier. My Father was the man I adored so much, and growing up, as he was 20 years my elder, he was the person I could confide in when I couldn't talk to my parents. My Mother, my best friend passing one year later same day, I believe, from a broken heart. It was a big decision to move. Evan and I were too committed with the move, and we needed to make it work.

The promises and deceit with the Hotel proposition started to unfold 12 months later. Even with profits coming through, the books weren't balancing. Then came the shocking news that the Hotel needed to go into liquidation, and we were left out in the cold.

Evan thought it best I return to my Fathers' with the boys. There were so many questions in my mind, like "would this be permanent?". On the upside, my Father was happy, and we were home.

A few months passed, and I settled back into city life, with late-night conversations on where to from here. Evan had moved in with an acquaintance, 'Cowboy' (more to follow) and then into his own home, trying to engage in a previous trade of house painting. I felt the distance forming between us. 'When are you going to come and visit'? I would ask.

A few months later 2 am one morning, a thunderous continual knock on the door, to be greeted by two policemen and the words you never want to hear. "Are you Mrs Mooy, Wife to Evan Darcy Mooy?".

"Yes, I am", I replied. Heart sinking, I heard the words 'We need to inform you, he is deceased." Did I hear that right? "Nooooo!" I screamed. "That's not right. I was speaking to him last night…". The last thing I remember was, 'let us escort you inside to sit down.'

I was so confused. The first thing I thought was that my baby boy didn't have a father anymore! I have since blocked out a lot, and the pain still is sharp.

I can't recall most of the events that followed, except travelling to where Evan was born, seeing his hometown, attending the funeral with some of his Family and Friends and feeling like an outcast at the funeral, especially with his Family. So many questions as to why he would take his life, and I could not find any words to explain the journey we had endured, especially to his son and daughter. I couldn't even look into their eyes. I felt all the questions pointed at me with insinuations that I must have known what was inside Evan's head. I did not. No words, silence.

They say time heals all, but I haven't found that to be true. They may become distant but never forgotten.

I found it hard to settle; wanting to walk the ground he had walked in his last days, a longing to hear or see anything to understand the decision that Evan must have made in his final hours, became too much, so we returned back to the Country. This time with my Father begging us not to go, but I needed to know why. I was now in the anger stage of grief, wanting answers.

Well, I never received those answers, yet my questions led me back to the kind, gentle 'Cowboy' named Ben. He had spent time with Evan. Did he know what he was going to do? Ben, at the time, experienced a dramatic divorce losing visiting rights to his three children, and our two Worlds merged. We were able to talk about our sorrows to one another, and the connection became strong.

He suggested we stay with him whilst looking for the answers. If I trusted him enough, he would ensure the boys, especially my Brad, only two years old, continued their School and routine feeling safe and secure whilst I occasionally visited my Father.

I had no friends in the Country, no one to rely on. That's when you grow up quickly and occasionally ask why I always have to be the strong one?

It was one of those trips to Sydney in 1990 when I came across a Decorative Art Exhibition, the colours, textures and subject matter pulled me in instantly, and I asked where I could learn more about this painting style. One of the Artists handed me a card before I realised I was on the phone asking if my soon-to-be teacher gave lessons? The answer was "yes!".

There is something about expressing and losing yourself with colour and form. I made a decision, with Ben's kind offer, I would travel back to Sydney weekly to commence an Arts Diploma and stay with my Dad.

The course was captivating, and I had talent, the formula for expanding entered my heart and mind. One day whilst back home, I took the pieces into a furniture store, expecting an opportunity to display, however, what came next blew me away. "Would you consider setting up a space in our store and conducting classes?"' Could I do that? The little voice inside me asked? The answer from Ben was "yes, you can!"

He was my greatest supporter with this and my next Business.

The word was out! The classes filled up quickly, and this decorative painting became the talk of the Town. No advertising spend was required, yet with that came the difficulty in sourcing supplies.

Ben's solution was to rent a shop and run the classes and supplies. The decision was made to go ahead, and in the first 12 months, rent was made over and over, more supplies were purchased, and the classes became so popular that students were on a waiting list.

Next was to buy our premises, extend if needed, and offer more classes. Ben became a master woodworker, a framer and a charming host. He devoted his life to my dream. We had an opening Gala Evening, and it was packed!

I loved my Business to the very core, and it never seemed like work, however, it became my obsession and my life needed to be balanced.

Ben became lonely and turned to drinking heavily, also suffering the loss of his Children weighed heavily as well. I was so self-absorbed with my classes and relationships. Honestly, I didn't see things as bad as they were.

In recent times I have learned that our actions heavily impacted the Boys. I started having requests to teach at other studios across the Country. I was excited at the opportunity. I was even asked to judge at the Sydney Royal Show twice! My Dad never got to see this success. He suffered a stroke in 2001, I brought him up to the Country, and he passed away shortly after. I am grateful we had the time together.

Josh got his big break too, with the opportunity to study at Sydney University. Money was available, and he never looked back.

Life was good until a hurdle with my health presented. " Mrs Mooy, that cyst on your back, the biopsy has revealed you have Melanoma"...." We recommend having conversations with your Family and Children in closing all loops and putting all your affairs in order."

Shock, disbelief, anger, sadness and tears are a few words to describe what I was feeling. I now had to ask, 'why me again?'. I was not prepared to accept this.

Then two things happened. Firstly, I began searching for clean products for my body and our household. Secondly, the Farm we bought of 4000 acres was still carrying a mortgage. The debt from purchasing beef cattle and registered bulls was excessive, and we were now at risk of losing the farm due to a crippling drought. Five-hundred thousand dollars in debt back in 2002 is a lot of stress.

Our tiny local paper had an advertisement section, and there I'd watch a 3 line advertisement that read, "Earn $500 - $1000 per month Working from Home part-time". I thought it was too good to be true; however, I dialled the number, and it reached a voicemail. I was sent a video to watch and some product samples to try, and I was blown away by both. Why had I not seen and tried this before?

I thought this was our way out of this mess, and the energy levels from these products and researching the ingredients ticked all the boxes for clean, responsibly sourced, and natural. Everything was in order. I carefully took the minimal start-up money ($90) from Josh's money box and left an IOU that read, I will pay this back to you tenfold and with that, I was so excited, I wanted to tell the World.

One problem, I was the pouncing Tiger, not the cool Cat. I kept hearing from my Mentors to keep using products and talking to people... so I did. Again, two things happened.

After attending my monthly check-up, I was heading to my 5th, and my Specialist said 'something is changing. Your bad cells are not multiplying and spreading. Are you doing something different we need to document" Immediately, I assumed this was my opportunity to help thousands of clients. No! However, the consistency of flyers in mailboxes, faxes to businesses, advertising everywhere small adverts in print, and morning tea presentations led to 45 clients and VIP clients in the first 90 days. The foundation of the Business came from those clients, and things were about to go nuts.

I attended meetings that were an 8-hour return trip monthly to learn as much as I could, and by 2008 I paid back the $90 by 10 to my Son, and there was mortgage being paid, food on the table, and the cupboard was full.

The little extras like the cost of sports or books for Josh at University could be paid. Life was becoming more manageable, and my happiness brought positive health results.

I thought, Wow! 6 years. Imagine what we can do in the next 6.

It was a Wednesday my Weight Loss Challenge class was on, and I was heading into Town. As I was heading down the drive, I thought, this is strange. Ben said he was breaking in a new horse. He's gone early, perhaps tired and forgot to close the horse paddock gate.

Meanwhile, the class was pumping. We were having a healthy morning tea, and my neighbour called me. 'The words I couldn't quite make out through the sobs, and Jason said, "Agi, I found Ben when I was riding on the top of the Mountain. It looks like he has come off his horse."

'Okay,' I said, "I'm here in Town. I'll call 000". "No, Agi! I've called the Police rescue. Come home. He's not breathing anymore."

I don't recall my Boys racing Home (Josh was now a teacher in Sydney with a beautiful Wife, Jane, and Brad, an apprentice Floor and Wall Tiler in Scone) or any of the funeral, except he was loved and there were 600 people packed into a rather small church.

Once I could think and speak again, through all the emotions, grief, sadness, and anger to understand I had my Life, my Boys and a Business with loving People around me that could keep us safe emotionally and financially.

3 Months after Ben's death, I poured my soul into my Business, helping hundreds of people make decisions, move forward, and better their lives, helping them understand no one was coming to save them. Only they could do that for themselves.

My income, passion and credibility exploded, taking me to many Countries. I spoke on many stages, with my largest audience being 23,000 in Bangkok. I had 14 paid Vacations and rose to the company's top 2% income earners.

They say everything that goes up must come down. Easier said at times because what was about to happen next kept me down for the next five years. It's all in how we handle things and constantly move forward.

My second grandson Luke, at the age of 10 weeks, developed a rare Tumour on his spleen, and at the time remember I was telling Josh, Luke's Dad, "God is good, and he is looking after us, Luke, will pull through this and Charlie will have his little Brother back."

Sitting in a Hospital room for the next four months, barely leaving, watching Josh, Jane and Charlie, cradling him, singing to him, with his little heart continuing to beat, and beat strong, but as each day went by, we were told the tumour became more and more aggressive, and treatment wasn't working. We took Luke out for the day to the Zoo, carrying him with all his drips and cords, my beautiful, beautiful Angel. Shortly after, we celebrated his six-month Birthday with cake. Days after he was Christened, we took the painted imprints of his tender little hands and feet. Not long after that, his little heart stopped beating. He was with God.

For five years, I was broken. I couldn't help anyone, not even myself. My now Husband Stephan was immensely supportive, yet even he couldn't get any spark to ignite me. You see, I never asked for help.

Brad, his beautiful Wife Michaela, and their two boys, Michael and Marcus, light me up. Josh, Jane, Charlie and Angel Luke are my World.

It's 2023; how did I get here, through all this?

I finally prayed for help.

The Teachers started appearing, Jan and Monika Zands, Ray Higdon, and then a miracle... Elsa Morgan and her Legacy Coaching System are helping thousands of Women accelerate in Business and Life. I was calling this in for 12 months, journaling. I embodied the system with such an appetite and success that I am now Staff with the Queenie Effect, passionate about our Clients' successes.

My Network Marketing Business this year celebrates 20 years and is growing.

I have never missed taking the products because I know I am here telling my story because of them.

I have a successful Clinical and Medical Hypnotherapy practice. Here, I can assist broken people, some who turn to substance abuse, and others needing to quit addictive behaviours, fear phobias and grief. Everyone has an opportunity to become 'unstoppable'.

The dress is now linen, not crepe, the hair auburn and flowing, here in my office sending all my love with these final words:

1. Never quit. Stay around the campfire.

2. You can't be for everyone, and everyone should not be for you. Do not dim your light for anyone. The door is for you to walk through first.

3. And a 'no' is not a 'no' forever; it is simply a 'no, not right now.'

4. Ask for help.

Just know always to remain grateful. You are not broken. You have been chosen to shine.

About the Author

Agi Mooy is Australian-born, with Hungarian parentage, living in the Hunter Valley of N.S.W. She is a Wife, Mum to a Family of Six, currently six Grandbabies with one Angel in Heaven and two Furbabies. Agi is a certified Clinical and Medical Hypnotherapist with qualifications in the Quit program, PTSD specialist and Ideal Weight. She is an onboarding Coach assistant for the Queenie Effect Company and also celebrating 20yrs as a Wellness Coach in the Nutrition and Fitness Industry.

Her greatest passion lies with assisting women like her to understand and break through their limiting beliefs, to enable them to embrace their Businesses and soar to heights they have only ever dreamt of. On any given recharge day, you will find her with her family, creating art, cooking, gardening and taking long walks along a beach. She is a true Taurean by heart and nature.

Email: agimooy@me.com
Facebook: www.facebook.com/agimooy
Instagram: www.instagram.com/mooy.agi

Andrea Stevens

From working full-time, to living the life of my dreams

I was 39 years old, facing the BIG 4-0. A life I loved, a life so rich in experience, in lessons, and in blessings.

My friend and I were talking at a yoga class for our two-year-olds. I questioned her, "What if I'm happy the way I am? This whole idea of "Made for More", the idea that there is something bigger out there, why can't I just be satisfied with my current life? Why can't being a Mom, a wife, a volunteer, and a community contributor be what I was meant to do?" I asked these questions sarcastically, somewhat rhetorically, equal parts offended and intrigued by this new movement. With our oldest children in school and our youngest kiddos posing in down-dog, I thought about my current life. I LOVED my freedom to get together with friends throughout my days, to chat, visit and support each other through motherhood.

I pondered this movement that was new to me. I wondered what's wrong with my life? I am so blessed to have a husband who works so hard so that I can stay home with my babies. We have food on our table, reliable cars, and had just purchased our very first home, a home that needed new flooring on every surface, paint on every wall, new electrical outlets, switches, and fixtures, all of which I did. I became a YouTube learner, laying almost 1,000 sq. ft. of flooring with my Best Friend in just 48 hours. I stayed up late and woke up early to paint every single wall in our house. I clipped wires and reinstalled all of the electrical outlets and switches to change from browns and creams to stark white. I figured out how to fix our ice maker, caulk the bathroom vanity, and completed a bathroom remodel, including tearing down wallpaper, patching and repairing drywall, texturing, and painting the walls. I did it all. I felt proud of my accomplishments. I did it in pockets of my time while my 2 & 6-year-old girls were running circles around me.

There were days I'd flash back…

Back to walking the streets of Mexico City, of Sailing in the San Blas Islands of Panama, or sipping Carmenere in Chile. I would think of the hundreds of students I'd taught over the years, many from wealthy Mexican or Colombian families. I would remember the funny stories, the awkwardness of middle schoolers, and the hours spent helping my students not only learn to like math, many found a love for it too. Riding the country roads in the Andes Mountains at 6:00 in the morning on a school bus filled with teachers from Colombia,

Canada, and the US, sharing stories and adventures, often traveling and exploring together on Holidays. It feels like another life. When I hear the stories come out of my mouth, it seems almost fake, made up, a dream. But it was so real.

In 2005, my then-fiance and I both graduated with our Master's in Art of Teaching (MAT) from a small private University. We got married six months later and took our five-year honeymoon three weeks after that. We started in Mexico, then on to Colombia. We explored and traveled a lot.

I recently pulled my entire stash of cloth diapers out of storage. I gave them so much power, it almost felt like a badge of honor to know that those 24 cloth diapers was a challenge that I conquered. Our oldest arrived one month early, making her only three weeks old when we moved 5 hours away so that my husband could go to Law School. We moved into Family Housing, lived on the 3rd floor walk up and had scored a three-bedroom apartment with 800 sq ft. Because we were relocating with a (tiny) newborn to a new town, the plan was for me to become a Stay at Home Mom (SAHM). I was terrified. Where was my social interaction going to come from? How was I going to work out? What about my Master's Degree? When would I go back to teaching? Who was I becoming?

We made so many sacrifices. We budgeted, used savings, my husband worked his ass off to earn scholarships. We decided to cloth diaper our baby, it sounded so gross, but after receiving 24 as gifts at our baby shower, realizing it would cost us nothing, it didn't sound so gross. I created a system, hooking up our tiny washing machine to the kitchen sink and washing eight at a time, every day, for three years. I had it down, but it took work, dedication, and determination. These diapers are a badge of honor. With pride, I passed them on to a sweet couple a decade and half our junior, expecting their first. As I rewashed, folded, and packaged them up, I felt like I was passing on a golden baton.

During the first few months of Law school, I found a coupon for a membership to workout with other new Moms while our babies sat in strollers. I met so many new friends, a new community and felt my confidence grow in motherhood. When my 30 days ran out, I knew our zero-income lifestyle could not afford to pay for my membership. So rather than quitting, I got certified to teach the classes! I became a certified fitness instructor for Pre and Post Natal Mothers. Not only did I not have to give up my new community, I got to teach new Mamas how to be active with babies in tow.

My daughter and I met some of our best friends in that setting, and both found a love of fitness, activity, and loving our bodies, something that was new to me. You see, I'd struggled with my body, treated it terribly, said some nasty things to it and about it. I'd fluctuate my weight 40+ lbs, both up and down, more times than I could count. The day my oldest daughter was placed in my arms for the first time, I looked at her face and her body and couldn't believe that something so perfect existed. That I had created her, grown her in my body, the same body that I had treated so poorly for 33 years, something so perfect came out of all my flaws. That day I vowed to never speak poorly about my body again. I vowed that she would NEVER hear me say something negative about my flaws. I would set the example of self-love, positive body image, and a healthy lifestyle. She was the most perfect thing on the face of this Earth, and she came out of my body, my body that was perfectly made to create her.

I wasn't new to the fitness world, I was a student-athlete, I had taught step and water aerobics in my early twenties, I'd joined gyms in most cities/towns I'd lived in, run some 5 & 10ks, and I generally liked to move my body, so teaching fitness classes wasn't entirely foreign to me. But my desire to help women feel confident in their bodies started to bloom. I started having conversations with women who were pregnant or had just given birth about loving themselves right where they were, that a "goal weight" isn't as important as self-care and self-love. I found a passion in helping women feel part of a community, a desire to be active, and the ultimate goal to set a healthy example for their young children.

After three years of Law School, my husband graduated Order of the Coif, meaning top 10% of his class. The sacrifices we had made had paid off! He had his pick of where he wanted to work, what kind of law he wanted to practice, and the lifestyle we wanted to live. A few things we had learned over those three years... 1) Time is a nonrenewable resource and our most precious commodity. 2) We could live on very little income. 3) We truly enjoyed our time together.

After exploring all of his options, digging deep into our vision of how we wanted to raise our family, we had to focus and prioritize. He could've started with a high-paying corporate job, with demanding hours to match; the big city life, fancy cars, a large home, and vacations. Large fancy firms were reaching out to him to interview, wine, and dine and get this top of his class guy to pick them. But we'd learned that money can't buy time, that we already had a three-year-old and another on the way, we knew that we could live a rich life without the long hours. And so, he landed his dream job, working in a rural county, as a prosecutor. They pay half as much, but the ability to clock out at 5:00 each day. He wanted to be home for dinner every night. It was important to us both that we sit around our table and connect, share, and laugh as a family. Time>Money.

So we made the 2.5-hour move away from friends, family, and the only life our three-year-old had ever known and started all over. I left my fitness instructor job that I LOVED so much. I nervously showed up at the library in our new community, craving friendship, connection, and playdates for my girl. Within weeks, we made some friends, within the year, we had a new baby and an entire new network of amazing people. We worked hard to build our community, to create an insulated village that was safe, secure, and positive to raise our girls.

December of 2018 came, we'd owned our home for six months, I'd worked tirelessly to update and make it a home. My oldest was in Kindergarten, where I volunteered 2+ times a week, I was Vice President of the PTA, and coached her soccer team. My youngest was 2, she kept me busy as most two-year-olds do, enjoying story and music times at the public library, toddler yoga, and a busy social calendar. I also was in my 3rd year of serving as the Secretary of the School Board at a local Preschool. I felt like I'd hit the jackpot. I was living the dream. I got to be home with my babies, socialize with my friends during the day, and workout (at home) whenever I wanted to! Life could not be any better! And so I questioned my friend, "why would I want more?"

Just days after the conversation with my friend, what would become the most life-changing decision happened because of a series of events. My husband, being a prosecutor, deals with, let's say, "criminal minds" he was on a particular case that made me nervous. One night I startled awake from a nightmare that involved me needing to cash in on his life insurance and finding a way to go back to work to support my fatherless children. I started researching what it would take to renew my teaching license. I started thinking about a backup plan. What would I do if the unthinkable happened? My husband reassured me I'd be fine and that nothing was going to happen. The very next morning, I scrolled across a post on the internet. The Topic: If you make money working from home, what do you do? There were hundreds of answers, most were Direct Sales companies I'd heard of, but one stood out to me…" I sell activewear"… I read it again, looked down at my OLD stretched-out leggings, readjusted my lack of support sports bra,,,,,,, and thought, hmmm…

I distinctly remember standing up and pouring myself a cup of coffee, and sitting back down, reading it again. I got up, walked to the kitchen, sat back down again, and decided to ask a single question. I sent this stranger a message, "Hi, I saw your comment. Can you tell me more about your activewear business?" I paced back and forth, waiting for her answer. I told her I wasn't looking for anything, that I was so busy. I'm an over-thinking, procrastinator and people pleaser, not a jumper. I take my time, think things out, and ask for other's opinions. Here I was with butterflies in my stomach, everything in my mind saying, this is crazy, you don't have time, what will others say? And yet, my heart was YELLING, "Do it. Do it now. Why not? Why not you? What's the worst that can happen?" I devised a plan to share this info with my husband when he got home, a way for his skeptical mind to get on board. I told him my idea, he questioned everything, and I looked at him and said, "give me six months, let's see what I can do." Within 24 hours of "meeting" this stranger on the internet, I JUMPED ALL IN.

I was so excited. I hadn't even touched the product, had no idea about the quality, but yet, I had the belief that my life was about to change. I just had NO idea the depth of it. Within the first month, I not only earned my original investment back, I doubled it. The following month I grew my team, earned customized Nikes and an Apple Watch, along with two different cash bonuses. My friends were seeing how much fun I was having. A few jumped with me, others watched skeptically, some thought I was crazy, while others cheered. I didn't care what they thought. I knew that I was representing an incredible product that I LOVED!

Within the first four months, I'd earned an all-inclusive trip to Cabo for my husband and me. I was ecstatic! Not only had I made a substantial income, I was fulfilling that passion to help women feel confident in their bodies. That same drive I had as a fitness instructor was coming back. Showing women that a pair of leggings can build your confidence was addicting. Leading, supporting, and encouraging women to start their own businesses, to make a difference for their families, and to change the future for themselves and their kids was incredibly fulfilling. 10 months into my new business, my husband and I left our kids for the first time ever to soak up the rays in Cabo. It was so surreal. On that trip, I realized how much I missed traveling.

The memories of living abroad for five years started flooding back, and my desire to explore this Earth was stronger than ever. It was then that I realized that yes, I lived a very blessed life as a SAHM. I also deserved to want more, to work for more, and to have more. Since then, I've traveled to Nashville, Salt Lake City (3 times), Southern California, I took my husband to Cancun, and we are off to Waikiki this year!. But that's not all; we've been able to go on some epic family vacations; I like to pay for the "fun stuff" for our family with my business. Trips to Disneyland, Legoland, Fairs, Every sport season (we do them all), and equipment. Because of my business, we have "fun money" to explore, to learn, and to grow. My girls and I do happy dances in our kitchen when someone new joins our team, or someone else hits a goal.

I had planned on going back to the classroom when my youngest started Kindergarten. The truth is, I don't want to miss a thing. I don't want to miss a field trip, a reading group, or an opportunity to help in their classrooms. I don't want to have to call in sick because I have a sick kiddo. I want to hop on a train or a plane to explore without asking permission. I want to experience all that I can with my kids because the years fly by, and time is our most valuable and nonrenewable resource. My business affords me the ability to do what I want when I want to because of the time and financial freedom. My business affords me a life without limits.

So, to that Mom standing over her two-year-old in toddler yoga class, the answer is this. It is ok to be happy where you are, absolutely. But don't close your eyes or ears to opportunity. There is something bigger out there. Being a Mom will be the BEST thing you ever do, but why not do it in the BEST way possible? Why not create a life with financial and time freedom? A life that affords you to live with abundance, without financial stress or having to get permission from your boss to let you go on a field trip or to stay home with a sick kid. I'm here to say that while I'm creating a dream life for myself, I'm taking 1,000s of women with me. We are setting goals, we are building each other up, and we are creating a life of freedom.

You are "Made for More". I encourage you to find a product or service you love and jump ALL in, don't stop to question.

Get excited and JUMP! Don't worry about what others are saying about you or to you unless they are uplifting and supporting you.

They don't get to have an opinion.

And finally, there will never be a time in life that you will feel "ready" or that you "know everything".

The amazing thing about starting a business and working towards time and financial freedom is that you learn as you go.

You WILL fall down, but you WILL get back up.

It is just like becoming a mother for the first time or the day you got married.

You have no idea what the future holds but always have faith that you will figure it out.

About the Author

Andrea Stevens is a leader in network marketing.

From sharing on virtual stages to one-on-one training, she strives to help women feel confident to lead an abundant life filled with adventure and freedom.

Andrea and her husband spent five years teaching middle school math out of the United States and have traveled much of Mexico, Colombia, and other Latin countries.

Now as a mom to two girls and a golden retriever, she spends her time building her business, volunteering in schools, and traveling as often as she can.

She is passionate about being active with her family and friends, specifically walking the beach, hiking in the woods, running an occasional ½ marathon, and playing and coaching volleyball (both sand and court).

In the summer, you'll find Andrea and her family learning to sail, camping in the woods, and on weekends, she takes the driver's seat of the family ski boat.

Email: zyiawithann@gmail.com
Facebook: facebook.com/andrea.s.blanc.5
Instagram: Instagram.com/annloveslife411

Bonnie Clark Harris

Overcoming Obstacles and Starting Over in My 50s

I never thought I would be starting my career over in my 50's, but there I was. How did this happen? One day I was a CFO of a successful aerospace welding company, and then after 20+ years, I found myself out of a job. Life is full of all kind of surprises. You never know what tomorrow will bring.

I was scared, angry, and felt lost all at the same time. I didn't know what to do. I knew the world had changed a lot, and the probability of someone hiring me without a college degree was very slim. The pay, the commissions, and all the benefits were gone. I had two choices, start at the bottom and work hard for someone else or start at the bottom and work hard for myself. I chose to invest in myself.

There happened to be another company that was getting ready to close its doors, so we met, and it seemed to be my chance to own my own business, and so I took it. In just 3 days, I went from an employee to an owner.

About 4 years into my entrepreneurship, my business was

doing pretty well. I was 44 years old, been married for 16 years, with two boys ages 11 and 6. Our world was about to be shaken. I was diagnosed with liver cancer. The news was devastating. It's difficult to describe what I was feeling the moment I got the call. Fear, shock, anger, disbelief, confused, but mostly terrified. My life was totally flipped upside down and would never be the same again.

I was so scared. I started thinking about what would it be like for my children to grow up without a mother. The fear of not seeing my children ever again and leaving my husband alone to raise our boys was almost too difficult to imagine. Suddenly I felt like I was all alone.

I couldn't do it. I refused to have this be my fate. I had so much to live for. Despite all the obstacles and challenges I was up against, I decided to fight. I would fight to live.

That's when I started to manifest my future life. I saw my children grow up, get married and start a family of their own. I saw my husband and I traveling to places all around the world. I started working hard on my mindset. Thinking only positive thoughts and letting go of the fear. I learned to control my emotions and trusted God to see me through. I knew if I could change my thoughts, if I could see my future self, maybe, just maybe, I could create a future with me in it.

My mom used to tell me all the time you can make yourself

sick if you tell yourself that you don't feel well. And you can make yourself well if you believe you are well.

I knew the odds of surviving liver cancer were slim. I had to push the fear aside and not allow stress to overcome me. The cancer was very aggressive and was growing fast. In seven months, it grew from the size of a grape to a football. There wasn't time for chemo or radiation. The only way to remove this massive tumor was to operate. After going through biopsies, MRI's and several surgeons (because not many surgeons wanted to take on this challenge), I found a doctor who would take my case. I was preparing myself to go through surgery. Getting my mindset right. Writing love letters to my boys just in case mommy didn't come home. Two days before going into surgery, my doctor called me and said he had a death in the family, needed to fly out of the country for five weeks, and would not be able to perform my surgery. I said to him that I wouldn't make it for five more weeks. He said that he knew that as well and said he was sorry as he hung up the phone. I was in shock. But I had no time to panic. I had to stay calm and find another surgeon.

I met with my internal medicine doctor the very next day, and he made a call to the best liver resection doctor in the area, who agreed to perform my surgery. He worked on me for 5 hours and removed 80% of my liver. Leaving left dozens of surgical clamps inside to hold me together. And a 13-inch scar as a sign of strength...the sign of a survivor.

Surviving cancer made me feel like the luckiest woman in the world. I was a walking miracle. Everyone from the doctors, the entire medical staff, and dozens of interns at the Keck School of Medicine all said so. My case was considered their #1 liver cancer survivor and was discussed at every Monday morning meeting for weeks. Their main task was to figure out how the hell a healthy 45-year-old woman with no cirrhosis of the liver, never exposed to hepatitis, rarely drank alcohol, didn't smoke, ate healthy, never used drugs, had ended up with a rare form of carcinoma that they never even heard of.

At one of my follow-up appointments, my doctor told me, "Bonnie, you don't drink a lot, you eat healthy, and you don't smoke. You really don't need to change anything except switch to nontoxic ingredients for your hair and skin. Your skin is the largest organ on your body, and what touches your skin absorbs into your bloodstream in under 30 seconds and filters right into your liver."

A few weeks later, I started to feel like myself again. I gained back my strength, energy and felt pretty good. Except for my hair. After going through cancer and menopause, my hair was left dry, brittle, and frizzy. My hair dresser tried everything, but nothing worked.

So, I was now looking for clean, nontoxic products that could bring my hair back to life.

Three months into my recovery, I returned to work, but it was never really the same. The economy had taken a hard hit, and the business was not doing well. We struggled for a few years, trying everything to ride it out. My paychecks were shrinking, and I was not bringing much home.

It was the end of 2016 when I took a good close look at my personal finances. I saw that there was a lot of money going out and not much coming in. I would lie awake at night worried how I was going to make this work. We had a little bit in savings. We were using up the money quickly. We were in trouble. I knew something had to change.

By this point, I had now been working for myself for 11 years and loved being my own boss. Honestly, the thought of working for someone else made me cringe. Once you get the feel of freedom working for yourself, you really can't go back to working for someone else. Of course, I would if push came to shove, but I was wanting to try something, anything else than getting a second "job". But what? What can I do? What skills do I have? What am I good at? I started reaching out to friends, family members, and FB groups, letting people know I was looking to make an extra stream of income.

I started praying intentionally every single day. God, I have faith and I trust you that everything will work out and you will open a door for me. I will be patient and trust in You. Every night for about 4 months, I prayed hard. I asked God to open my eyes to new opportunities. To give me guidance.

One day, I saw my niece post a picture on social media. She was at a gorgeous mansion outside in front of a swimming pool with about 60 other women. They were all dressed in white and smiling. They looked so happy, and they were talking about being around successful people and building a community. I was interested in learning what this was all about.

I contacted my niece, and she invited me to a "Wash and Wine" event. That's where they pour you a glass of wine and shampoo your hair. It sounded like fun, and my hair needed a wash, so I accepted the invite. There were a dozen women who were attending the party, and one by one, they lined up to get a "hair spa" treatment. There were all different ages of women and all different types of hair. Fine, thick, frizzy, curly, wavy, thinning, coiled, bleached, blond, brunettes, every type! I was very skeptical how ONE brand of shampoo could help such a diversified group of heads of hair.

What I witnessed blew my mind!!! After just ONE wash, thin fine flat hair had a full body and was bouncy. Frizzy hair was smooth and tame. Curly hair was defined. Bleach blonds had a ton of shine!!! What in the world is this "Magic Shampoo" made of? I was shocked! I wanted to do some more research about the brand and the company first.

I went home, and I could NOT stop talking about this damn shampoo to my husband. Day and night, I talked about it. Light bulbs kept going off in my head. It is SHAMPOO. Everyone washes their hair. It is a CONSUMABLE product. They will use it and need to buy more. It is a NECESSITY. Everyone needs to wash their hair. When times get bad, and you have to cut things out to save money, people are not going to give up washing their hair. Shampoo is just as important as toilet paper, and we all know during 2020 how valuable a roll of toilet paper became.

A fire was brewing inside me. It was like I found a Golden Ticket. Was this what I had been searching for?

The company that I was thinking about joining had incredible products that were vegan, cruelty-free, non-toxic, smelled amazing, and even meet the stringent guidelines and clean ingredients standards of the European Union. They also help communities all over the world through their Gratitude programs. This was definitely something that I could get behind and support.

But, when it came time to push the button to join, fear started to set in. What if? What if this doesn't work? What if I can't do this? What if no one will see the vision like I do? I started to pull away and talk myself out of it. Then my husband intervened. He said, "Babe, I have NEVER seen you get so excited about something like this EVER!! I think you should really do this. What IF it does work out? What IF you do have success? If you don't, so what! You go back to doing what you were doing. But, if you don't at least give it a try, you will never know, and you will regret it for the rest of your life." He was right. I needed to stop listening to my head and go with my gut. I had this overwhelming pull to do it. A very calm feeling like everything was going to be okay. I literally felt like God was saying, "Bonnie, TRUST Me, this is the answer to your prayers. This is going to change your life, your family's life, and impact the world with your story."

So, I looked at my husband and said, "What should I do?" He tossed his credit card at me and said, "Buy the biggest product pack you want. I want you to do this. This is going to help us so much. I believe in you." So, I did.

I had no experience in sales. No Instagram account. I had 200 Facebook followers and zero influence. But I had passion, had excitement, and I saw the vision. I believed it was possible, and that is all I needed to get started.

So, I started to dig in and learn about my business. The more I learned from my back-office training, the more I fell in love with this brand. I took and passed all of their certification programs to not only educate myself but to provide the best possible service to my customers and provide value to my team.

I was coachable and willing to do things that made me uncomfortable. I knew success would take me getting out of my comfort zone and do things I have never done before. "If you want something you've never had, you must be willing to do something you've never done." – Thomas Jefferson

If I wanted this "side gig" to pay me like a real career and not like a hobby, I needed to treat it like a business and become a professional.

I started listening to podcasts and audiobooks like: Go Pro by Eric Worre and Go For No by Andrea Waltz, Ray Higdon, and Richard Fenton. Those 2 books helped me to launch my business.

I connected with our top leader Jewely Stephens in my company, and shared with her some of the things that I was doing to move my business. She was so impressed that she asked me to do a team training. This really helped build authority and my confidence. Others started to see me as a leader. It is pretty awesome how you can have a positive influence on others with your actions. I have had dozens of others reach out to me and share how I inspired them to go online and do a live video.

After working for about four years in my online business, I

found that I hadn't promoted passed a certain rank nor earned any passport trips. I realized that I could only go as far as I was developed.

I can distinctly remember sitting at my kitchen table and crying because I didn't know what the formula was for making a change. I needed to figure this out.

Once I realized that it was up to me to make a decision, to take control of my life, I decided to get to work.

I got smart and learned really fast, and I became obsessed with knowledge and getting better. I had a burning desire that this time I wasn't going to let anyone or anything stop me.

Once it became clear to me that I was choosing to be unstoppable, I had a clear vision of exactly what I wanted.

I hired a business coach. Her name is Elsa Morgan. She is the "No BS coach." She tells you like it is. She helped me by holding me accountable and sharing her simple system that I followed every day. And it worked! What I couldn't achieve by myself in four years I achieved by following Elsa's system in 9 months! I ranked up to the top 3% of my company and earned an all-expense paid trip to the Bahamas for me and my husband.

I have been able to bring in a steady income for my family because I was brave and clicked "join now". I get to plan, pay for, and even earn annual family trips to places like Cabo San Lucas, Las Vegas, and the Bahamas. Now I am on a mission to help other women do the same.

One way I am helping other women find the same success is when I met Perla. She was experiencing postpartum hair loss and was looking for hair products to help regrow her hair that she had lost from having her daughter. She was a bit skeptical but was open to giving the products a try. After trying the products and also realizing there was an opportunity to earn an income while she shared the products and her amazing results with friends and family, she decided to upgrade from a customer and become a business partner of mine. I helped her throw her first "Wash and Wine" party the following week. She was able to earn back four times her initial investment in her first month of signing up. Since then, Perla has promoted a few times and grown her business substantially. This extra income has really helped Perla's family and fill in the gaps of their budget.

If you're in a situation where you know you need to make changes, here are three suggestions I can share with you to help you:

- Start before you are ready. The lightness of being a beginner is exciting and frees you to be creative.

- Who loses if you don't make any changes? Your

children? Your spouse? Your parents? Your community? What will they have to live without, because you stayed exactly where you are right now?

- What if this does work? What if you are successful? What if you can achieve everything you have ever wanted because you decided to get up and try?

Believe me, I never thought in a million years that I would be traveling the world with my husband, helping hundreds of women start a business, acquiring hundreds of customers, and having the opportunity to leave a legacy for my children.

But here I am.

If a 57-year-old cancer survivor with ZERO experience can achieve this, so can you. I'm not promising it is easy, but I can promise it is well worth it. This is why I have overcome all of the obstacles and challenges that I faced in my life to pursue my life purpose and make a positive impact.

New beginnings can occur at any age. There is no limit to how much we can grow, learn, and become better people. Any decade in life provides an opportunity for self-improvement and growth. It wasn't my plan to start over in my 50's, but I have discovered that I am more than capable of making a living doing what I love.

Bonnie Harris

About the Author

Bonnie Harris is a 16-year entrepreneur growing a global online business for the past five years in the network marketing profession. In 2022, she reached the top 3% of her network marketing company and consistently places on the top leaderboards. She grew up in Azusa, California, and is married to her soulmate and best friend for 29 years.

She's a mother to a sweet angel in heaven and two incredibly talented boys. Rock concerts are one of her favorite pastimes. She has seen close to 300 bands to date. She is also a liver cancer survivor, and whole heartedly believes that this second chance has directed her to live life to the fullest and go after her dreams with purpose and intention. She is passionate about sharing her knowledge and experience to help women achieve their entrepreneurial dreams.

Email: bonnieharris427@gmail.com
Facebook: www.facebook.com/bonnie.clarkharris
Instagram: www.instagram.com/socalbon/

Bwalya Desmond

From Rock-bottom, to the top

In 2008 Tim and I celebrated ten years of marriage.

Like most couples, we had a lot of "stuff." We had cars, boats and mortgages, and like a majority of people, we didn't own any of it- the banks did. We were over-leveraged, but we thought that way of living was normal because we didn't know any different. We were unfamiliar with what it meant to budget, and we never tracked our income, let alone our expenses. We felt the pinch of having more "month than money" but were never compelled to do anything about it. We were only a $500 emergency away from not being able to cover our monthly bills.

Eventually, I saw an ad at our church for a class called Financial Peace University. I quickly signed us up for the 13-week course without discussion. We were finally presented with an opportunity that would help us put our finances in check and lead us towards a life of freedom from debt. We attended classes and gained knowledge about the basic financial principles on how to go from "more months than money" to having a plan in place and even paying off some debt! Through this, we gained the knowledge to be able to pay off $19,000 in debt, of which $12,000 was credit card debt. Paying off this debt was the beginning of hope. What we did not anticipate, however, was the obstacle that we were going to face two months after we paid off this debt.

I remember Tim coming home and telling me that he had been furloughed from his job with no certain date of return. How could this be happening? Fear and uncertainty gripped me, and I wondered how we were going to survive this. Our safety net of credit cards was no longer an option, as we had cut up our credit cards. I felt the control slipping from me, and there was not a thing I could do about it. Our two young boys were both under the age of six. We had three mortgages, car payments on both vehicles, a boat payment as well as daycare expenses. Our total debt was over $300,000. I found my mind racing night after night, searching for a solution or a way out. One particular night, I looked at Tim and asked how we were going to do this. I wouldn't say I liked the situation we found ourselves in. Who was to blame? How did we get here? This was my rock bottom.

What I knew with certainty was that something had to change. I didn't sit back and wish for something to happen. Instead, I took action. The next eight months were all about survival. I worked seven days a week, five of which were at my 9-5 job. On weekends, I worked as a server, catering events. I didn't shrink back and wait for my husband to figure something out. I dug deep within the survivor in me and did not entertain any thoughts that tried to tell me otherwise. I knew how to do hard things. I had faced tougher things alone, and now I had a partner. I gave myself permission to sacrifice for a little while so that we could have flexibility in our finances when Tim was called back to work. We were both willing to switch roles.

So, Tim took care of the house and everything to do with the boys while I kept a roof over our heads. I pictured in my mind what our reality would be if we did nothing. I didn't look at the eight months I sacrificed working two jobs as me missing out. Instead, I saw each day of taking consistent action as days leading us to our life of freedom that we so craved at this point. This, to me, was the only thing that mattered. It was not about what people thought or how it looked from the outside. We were doing what we needed to do for the survival of our family. We were responsible for our little humans. My fuel was the fear of getting behind in our mortgage and having to look at my boys and telling them that we had to move. Was this easy? Not at all. It required me to be someone I had never been before.

I drew a line in the sand and said out loud, "I will never be caught unprepared ever again".

Using the principles we had learned from the course, we mapped out a ten-year plan for us to become debt free. One of my mentors, Ron Reynolds, says that "Debt Freedom is the single freedom that makes all other freedoms possible.".

I spent many nights flat on my face seeking God's wisdom to help us stick to the plan. We needed a monthly miracle to pay the mortgage. The unemployment check could barely cover a utility bill. As time went on, we saw God's faithfulness displayed in our lives. We did not miss a single payment and honestly couldn't track where funds came from to meet the needs. We also remained faithful to tithing 10% of our income, and we surrendered it all to God. He was our source. We had to keep the boys in daycare to hold our spots since Tim's employer did not give him a definite return date.

In the beginning of this journey, we needed help embracing the idea of a budget. We felt like we were being controlled and like we were being told what to do with our hard-earned money. We feared living a life of complete restrictions.

What shifted for us was that we were willing to leave our old way of dealing with our finances behind.

We had weekly meetings that we called "board meetings" to hold us accountable to staying on track. The first few were not easy. We avoided eye contact to not let each other see the disappointment and shame that we felt for how we ended up here in the first place. We were on an obsessive mission to stay on track on our journey to debt freedom, but it did not come without obstacles.

We had challenges with tenants defaulting on rent payments and destroying our property which required us to spend thousands of dollars to fix, and our cars needed mechanical work. The ultimate blow came when we were at a neighbor's cabin for a fun weekend on the water. Tim had to work the night before and joined us early the next morning. Tim, for years, was a professional water-skier, and the opportunity for him to ski was something he couldn't pass up. He was eager to ski and quickly got himself changed and ready to go for a barefoot run. It was then that the inevitable happened, and a fluke accident changed it all. I remember the boys running into the house and yelling for me to come outside right away. They said that something had happened to dad and I had to come. In disbelief, I said really, what could have happened? He just arrived. He had literally done this a thousand times throughout the years without incident. The panic in their voices made me run out while I was still in my pajamas and slippers.

I ran to the edge of the dock and could see Tim standing in the water. I hollered to him and asked how he was doing. From where I was standing, I could not see anything wrong with him. He quietly said he needed a minute to catch his breath.

After what seemed like the longest minute, he tried to walk towards the dock and discovered that he couldn't. It was then that we decided to call 911. The 911 responders came with a backboard and managed to carefully lay him down. I could see tears streaming down the faces of the boys. I followed the ambulance with the boys to the local hospital. The CAT scan revealed a compression fracture of his T-5 vertebrae. He had broken his back. The hospital was too small to handle his diagnosis, and since we could not lay him in the car, Tim was transported by ambulance to our local hospital, which was 65 miles away.

This began a long journey to recovery for Tim. The great news was that he did not need surgery. His options were to have vertebroplasty (an injection which would help rebuild his vertebrae). This came with risks, one of which was the substance used in the injection was a known carcinogen. That was eliminated, as option two was a better option -go home and get flat in bed and take the load off your spine. He opted for the safer option, which was limited mobility through rest.

Our home was instantly transformed into an infirmary. Now our familiar scene was a walker, a grabber to put shoes on, or any household items that he needed when he was alone. However, a toilet seat riser became the popular item. Not only did it aid in Tim's recovery, but it has also helped several friends who have needed it through their own health setbacks.

Tim quickly learned to be independent and, within a few weeks, was able to walk around the block. Physical therapy enabled him to gain strength and hope to again be able to do the things he once did with ease. This journey that began as a normal day in July culminated in November when Tim passed his return to work physical. He was now able to lift 50 lbs, climb a ladder, bend and touch his toes, and not rely on prescription medications to get through the day. Through all of this, God was faithful.

What was meant to be a setback in our financial journey to debt freedom was minimized because of preemptive planning. We had chosen a supplemental insurance plan that would become effective after 30 days of being on short-term disability that we took advantage of. Health insurance covered most of the medical bills, except for deductibles, which were minimal in contrast to the total overall medical costs. We were finally in a good place to handle the unexpected emergency.

We had grown so much from the time we had started our debt freedom marathon. We had learned the power of working together as a team and the importance of holding each other accountable to stay the course. The Dave Ramsey course had taught us how to budget and to use the envelope system, which is what we have been using since 2008, and they had now become second nature. Going through the setbacks reminded us of why it was necessary for us to keep going. We spoke often about how we were going to feel when we paid off our first mortgage. We were doing the debt snow ball of paying our smallest debt first and taking that money and applying it towards the next bill, all while securing an emergency fund that was at least three to six months of expenses in savings.

Discipline was a key ingredient to our success. We knew that we couldn't get it done without sticking to the plan, being diligent, and staying the course without worrying about the short-term results. We knew the power of compounding. Zig Ziglar states, "If you do the things you need to do when you need to do them, then someday you can do the things you want to do when you want to do them."

As time progressed, our emotions also changed. We had gone from being led by fear and anxiety from being caught unprepared to having confidence in the plan that we had in place and the money saved up in our emergency fund to having hope of one-day becoming debt free and really accomplishing it. We had peace at night when we went to bed.

How we handle money impacts every part of our lives. We learned early in this process that Tim is a spender, and I am a saver. We had to work together as a team to have a successful outcome. I discovered that having money meant security to me. As our bank accounts grew, I felt cared for. We had power in unity. We made decisions together about major purchases and were both ok with the person who was more gifted at doing the budget and being in charge of paying the monthly bills.

A budget was essential for our success. Being on board together was critical and brought strength to our marriage. We learned to do a zero-based budget every month, meaning that we spent every dollar of our paychecks on paper first to eliminate the temptation of spending on non-budgeted items. We both agreed to making some shifts to help us. We established what was a true need versus a want. This led us to eliminate eating out for an entire year and only taking vacations once we could pay for them.

We knew that something had to give. We decided that these two things were important to us, and eliminating them for a short period of time so that we would be able to add them back was the way to go. We couldn't keep all things the way that they used to be.

Only some people that you tell about your journey will believe that you will actually achieve what you set out to do. I remember going to the bank every Friday to make a principal payment and my co-workers teasingly saying, "It must be Friday!" I re-assured them that one of these Fridays, I would be making my last mortgage payment.

On May 15th, 2016, that dream came true. We made our last mortgage payment- we were debt free! To say it was the greatest feeling is an understatement. Besides giving my life to Jesus and becoming a Christian and the days that my boys were born, this was the single best feeling in the world. The sense of freedom was something hard to describe. I felt like a load was lifted off my shoulders, and the shackles were removed. No one could ever take our home from us, no matter what we were facing. It gave me a great sense of confidence and tremendous peace. I wanted to shout this from the rooftop.

When I look back on our journey that started out as a wake-up call to the careless way that we ran our finances (without a plan and without an emergency fund), to where we were and accomplishing it in only eight years versus the ten years that we had planned on, it was a small sacrifice to make.

Our boys decided that basketball was their choice of sport. Being debt free allowed us to say yes to all the AAU sports that they wanted to do every summer that cost us thousands of dollars over the years. We could take vacations when we wanted to, and it allowed us to contribute to organizations that we believe in. We were also able to teach others the same principles that we learned so others could also have the same freedoms for their families.

We have come to believe that not only is it necessary to know your financial affairs, it is crucial to have an emergency fund in place- it is inevitable that you will face an emergency at one point. If you truly want to get out of debt, it is possible with a decided heart, a plan in place, and 100% commitment.

About the Author

A Native of Zambia who now resides in Wisconsin, Bwalya is a wife to her husband Tim and mother to Victor and Simon.

She is a certified John Maxwell coach and has an online health & wellness business and equips people to gain financial wealth & freedom in the network marketing space.

A lover of Jesus, Bwalya has a passion to inspire, encourage, provide hope, and lead others to a relationship with Christ.

In 2020, she created Bwalya's voice, where today, her encouraging and uplifting messages can be found, as well as on a variety of social media platforms.

To get started on your own journey to saving money, debt freedom, and wealth creation, let's Connect!

Facebook: www.facebook.com/bwalya.desmond
Instagram: www.instagram.com/bwalya.bchick/
TikTok: www.tiktok.com/@bwalyadesmond

Christine McFarlane-Olsen

A Train Station Called Dysfunction Central

At the Station

I have many memories of the boarding house I grew up in as a small child. I remember having my baths in the concrete washtub where all the tenants washed their clothes. I remember the little mice that would run around the room at night looking for crumbs to eat as I went to sleep on the couch that was my bed. One night when my mother cooked dinner, it was one egg in a frying pan with a bit of butter for us to share, and we had one piece of bread each. My mother cried as we ate. The most memorable dish that my mum would make was a broth with beef bones and weeds we foraged for around the house we moved to after the boarding house.

My childhood memories are filled with horrors I could not interpret as a child. The sexual abuse I suffered was at the hands of my father. I have no memories of when it began. It always was. I remember the day I thought to myself, 'hmm this is not right'. I was under five years old and not going to school yet. I grew up in a home with deep and dark pain. We were at a train Station called dysfunction central. It was a joke I developed in my late teens, and when I settled into long-term counselling after some months, the counsellor told me she thought I was exaggerating when I first started, but now, she said it had been completely accurate.

When I was 11 years old, I went to my father's house, as required by the court settlement, for a visit over the Christmas holidays, and I was allowed to have one of the other Farmers' kids over for the night. I thought awesome he'll leave me alone tonight. After dinner, I did the dishes, and as I left the dining room, I saw my friend curled up on the end of my father's bed, laughing and chatting with him. I flipped out and said, 'NO, Dad! You keep away from my friends and me. It can never happen again!'. Years later, I discovered he was paying her and had paid her to get the three of us into bed for the night. From around this time, I started acting out subtly at first, worsening over the next 15 years as I became depressed, suicidal, and addicted to alcohol and a range of drugs. I was arrogant, aggressive unstable, anti-social or friendly, calm, caring, supportive or miserable, staying in bed crying, in a fetal position, emotionally eating, and anaesthetising with more drugs and alcohol. I was all over the place and just went with the craziness, unable to control or change my feeling state from one moment to the next.

I grew up in trauma. I grew up in fear. It was ingrained in me by society, my community, my family, and my parents, verbally and by example. All of it was emotional, physical, and sexual, living it, surrounded by it, witnessing it, experiencing it, powerless, isolated and living in my head.

Surprisingly, the strength of your mind helps you to survive what you are living. Survival tactics take over, and how you think is changed. How you feel about family, how you think of relationships, other interactions, social services, police, government agencies or departments, your perceptions of yourself, your looks, your weight, your style, your education, where you grew up, your culture or mix of, how you see yourself in-light-of what you have always known. There was not one level, thought pattern or area of my life that was not impacted.

I have spent my life looking for healing, looking for safety, looking for belonging, looking for peace, looking for love, looking for joy, looking for pride, looking for the meaning of family, looking for success, all things that were foreign to me.

Over the years, I have seen many counsellors and doctors. The first doctor I spoke to told me he was deeply sorry, but he could not handle what I was telling him, and he recommended I see someone else. He had yet to learn that after that appointment, it was more than ten years before I sought help again.

The next counsellor told me that she could not help me to

change my feelings and that I would always be a slave to the destructive mental war of PTSD. Now I had a diagnosis. This was the issue, but it did not change anything in my daily life.

A few short years later, my mother passed, and I was desolate in grief when I returned to counselling again. My beautiful mother had died, yet here, my abusers lived. I found an amazing woman, one of the many earth angels I have met along my journey, TS, who would be my counsellor for many years through my grief for my mother. A significant amount of healing comes from opening up, naming, and acknowledging the realities of experiences and the change within us as a direct result.

There was still more trauma to come as life happened to all of us. This time there were medical issues for my family. My partner of 30+ years, father to my children, became sick with brain tumours and on his adrenal Gland. The brain tumour was removed and left him with life-changing emotional challenges. Meanwhile, the endocrinologist told us not to worry as the adrenal tumour was benign and not releasing any hormones. We were told that it would be fine and no longer needed to continue to do follow-up checks anymore.

Two years later, that same endocrinologist told us,' I'm so sorry, it's inoperable and terminal. You will die within 12 months.' We told the doctor we were getting married a week and a half later, and as we left, she told me she hoped we had time for the wedding. We cared for him at home. That was his wish. Hospice came to our home and supported us in his care. I learnt how to put in subcutes lines so we could make memories for our eight children. The youngest was two years old, and the oldest was 24.

His being at home allowed us to organise medication and visit his hometown. His sisters organised a Bach home for a few days, and we all stayed. Relatives came to visit. The children played on the beach. We drove down old roads, past old schools, old homes, and old pub haunts. We shared stories from old memories before heading back to hospital appointments and the exhausting job of caring for your loved one as they were ready to pass.

After the brain tumour surgery, I felt he was different. The vulnerability he felt was overwhelming because of the medications he was on. He had hallucinations, and his sense of time and memory had been affected. He often felt he couldn't trust what he remembered or what people told him. His sense of loss was significant from being a hardworking, strong, intelligent man. The emotional fallout of that came down primarily to me shouldering it. I had PTSD and was in bad shape. He didn't want to leave my side because I was sick, so we looked for solutions, strategies, and healers' natural herbal remedies' and sought out groups online for support.

Now, as a grown woman with a growing family of my own and

a sick partner whose life expectancy was soon (at best ten years), we also supported our daughter Ataahua, who had been having tests since age two because she developed ataxia tremors which affected all physical movement including fine and gross motor skills. She stopped speaking and had global developmental delays.

After seven years of tests, we received another medical blow to our family Ataahua was diagnosed with Mitochondrial disease. This was confirmed by an MRI scan of her head and torso, which showed she had a stroke-like event they estimated two years previously. A classic symptom of Leighs disease is a stroke-like event. At this stage, we had been with the metabolics' specialist team for some years, and I had researched this disease or genetic spelling mistakes, as our regular specialist called it. The truth is this disease is so terrible with little research worldwide at that time, no current medications available, and vitamin supplement treatment with zero guarantees that it would help or slow and certainly not stop any symptom.

Leigh's disease, as a diagnosis, hits you like a death sentence. It floors you. Every mitochondrial Disease patient can present differently, even between siblings with the same genetic fault. My two eldest daughters were diagnosed as adults after muscle biopsies were taken. The very basic explanation of mitochondrial disease is that the mitochondria are within every cell of your body and regulate energy to allow each cell to do its job. Cells cannot perform their job when there is a fault in the process. It can affect any organ. There is more research happening around the world now. Drug trials are being run on certain specific mitochondrial mutations, and none are happening in New Zealand.

I was devastated and would often cry over the next couple of years, and one day I thought, how dare I cry here in self-pity for a loss that hasn't happened yet. I wasted the moments we had to share love, laughter, and life. I struggled with her education and medical specialists' appointments but focused on planning and creating experiences. Her eating schedule had to be more regular. She had a snack alarm on her Ipad that would remind her teachers that she may need to eat. The specialist told us she could have many events over her lifetime, and being young, her body could heal from many things. She has recovered a lot from the cognitive effects of her event at age 7. She has developed seizures which the doctors have said are expected to progress, so we have to take it one day at a time. I am so grateful every day for the blessings I have Ataahua and her sisters are blessed. They can walk, talk, and breathe without extra oxygen and do not need regular suction to clear their throat.

Fast forward a little, and we had just done a local paper piece on Mitochondrial Disease for International Mitochondrial

Disease awareness week. A weekly magazine picked up the story and paid us for it. I wanted to do something beneficial with the money. I decided to buy into a business where I could work from home around all the health issues I was dealing with and help us get the food and supplements I felt the children needed. Next was to decide which one, so I researched different online companies and eventually joined one. I had never been in the online space before and had no clue what I was doing. I didn't like people as I was so withdrawn I didn't even like looking at myself in the mirror; what was I thinking, right? After I had joined online, I was assigned a coach to help me grow my business.

Enter stage right, AM. AM was great. I was resistant to her instructions and methods, and I'm sure she was frustrated more than a few times. I would start to do work and make progress, and then old habits and old patterns of thinking would jump out of my head, so I would drop off all the time with no follow-up or follow-through.

There was no way she could have known what I was going through.

AM would always follow up and reach out to me even when I let my membership lapse. She reached out at the beginning of 2022. I had been in the business for five years and had not moved grown and was only buying for myself. I was living in a 3-bedroom home with my eight children.

My bedroom was the lounge area at home, and I shared this space with my 26-year-old daughter and 6-year-old son. We barely had room to put our feet on and walk around our beds. We needed more room for a desk or a dedicated office work area. I had a library, which I loved, so I made space on the existing bookshelf. When I joined a zoom or online training, I had my phone propped up against a bottle of sanitiser on top of a paint bucket. Agi messaged me one day and said I am in this fantastic group for women who want to grow their business online; you should jump and see what you think. So I did.

I joined the Legacy Academy and committed to doing the work daily.

I was so amazed. This is what I was looking for. They talked about who you needed to become and how to work on yourself then my aha moment came. If your environment is not right, you will never be successful—boom, no organised space, nowhere for creative energy to flow. I knew then that it was time. As devastating as it might feel for my children to leave their childhood home filled with love and memories, I had to move. All my children have struggled since their father's death. It was time for our health and for us to move forward as a family from the past hurts into a healthier home where we can grow and begin to live, not just survive. I wanted so much more for my children and knew it had to come from me.

Another gem that hit me from training as you need to get your head right. You can't fake it. You need to do the work on yourself, whatever that is. And that hit me, and I knew I had so so much more work to do. I already knew that I was still living, controlled by my depression cycle, and I was falling fast.

Restrictions from the pandemic were starting to lift, and I knew the Psychologist on the metabolic team, so I asked to see her. I felt like I might need medication. My regular doctor had retired, and the new doctor wanted me to see the mental health team at the hospital. The crisis team took a month, and my appointment was pushed out twice, and then they had to see their supervisor. During this time, as I had no other help, I began meditating daily, walking in nature daily, surrounding myself with only positive people, and focusing on looking after myself for my family. Part of the daily routine also included legacy training. If you want something different, you need to do something different. I needed more work on myself to discover what I could be, something I still needed to do.

And then, the blessing presented a beautiful and trusted friend who became qualified as Clinical Hypnotherapist. I reached out, and my sessions were booked. After the regression therapy sessions, I cannot articulate fully how it felt. I have since decided it is because I had never felt that way before.

I am so excited about all my accomplishments since starting at the Legacy Academy. In 12 months, I have moved to a beautiful 2-level, five-bedroom, three-bathroom home. It is so far from the concrete tub in a boarding house that I remember from childhood. I am a co-author in a book about unstoppable women, I am investing in me to grow me, I am backing me (and for once, I believe it), and I have been blessed with the opportunity to purchase a 5-acre block of land which I signed for during the writing of this book. We are ready to develop it in the first 60 days of 2023.

My planning for the year, each month, every week and daily routines have never been so strong. I can feel the habits becoming easier. I am levelling up what I am. I can feel it. I want to keep growing and create peace, abundance and fulfilment of all my goals, dreams and desires. Writing and having my story published is a long-time dream from when I was around 17 years old that somehow my story could help someone else hold on, move on, reach out, and want more. I am in a season of no, and anything/anyone that does not align with my vision for the future will not have space at my table. I am attracting other women who are also beginning their journey with me.

My vision is to share what I have learnt firsthand in changing blocks women may have holding them back—allowing them to live their life to the fullest.

IF YOU BELIEVE YOU CAN, YOU CAN, AND IF YOU BELIEVE YOU CAN'T, YOU CANT.

Strategies I have used:

- Reach out to someone you trust.

- Journal negative emotions as you feel them, then release them.
- Spend time in nature, walk barefoot on grass or at the beach, and move your body.
- Start a gratitude journal at the beginning of the day to get your focus positive.
- reprogram negative internal dialogue with positive affirmation meditations.
- Eat well. It is a form of self-love.
- Help someone else.

About the Author

Christine McFarlane-Olsen is 51 years old, born in Auckland, New Zealand, and of Maori descent.

She grew up in west Auckland, and after a few years working in the central suburbs of Auckland, she moved back west to bring up her family. Christine left school without qualifications as a teen returning at age 25 to complete her form 6 certificate with two children under three and very few support systems in place.

She is a survivor, and she is living life. Her vision for the future is to empower and inspire women to live their lives to the fullest. It's never too late to have another goal or to dream another dream.

Facebook: www.facebook.com/profile.php?id=100007173003270

Instagram: www.instagram.com/herbalmama_christine_mcfarlane/

Deneen Iverson-Kidd

Becoming the best version for my vision, my family & me

I grew up fatherless.

My mom and dad were married, but I don't remember him ever living with us. I don't recall doing family "things" with him at all.

The only conversation I remember having with my father was when on one of his visits, he basically told me I was fat and needed to lose weight.

I told him that I made the high school volleyball team, and he said," You should play softball. That will help you have a smaller waistline." I don't remember how I felt before he said that. I don't even remember how I felt afterwards. What I do know is that everytime he visited after that-I hid. I hid behind a neighbor's home and ignored my mom, sister, and brother calling out my name until I knew he was GONE.

Looking back, I believe that was the beginning of my struggles with my weight. Food was my best friend and eating lots of it was the comfort and love I never received from my father.

I continued to hide as well. I hid my feelings. I didn't speak my mind. I loathed arguments and confrontation. And I hid behind my fat.

I was the quiet, studious child who hid behind books yet dreamed of being an actress. I pursued acting in junior high and high school but always found a reason to quit. I remember saying to myself, "You are too fat and black to be in movies!"

I went to college because it was expected of me. I did well in high school-so what else was there to do? I tried to be the "good girl"-I didn't want to cause any trouble for my mom. She was doing the best she could for us and was a good mother.

I earned a degree in Marketing from Pennsylvania State University, but I have yet to really work in the field. I worked as an inside sales representative and in retail for several years but found that it wasn't very fulfilling.

The strong relationships I had with younger cousins, nieces, and nephews led me to going back to school to get my teaching certificate. Teaching was challenging, long hours, and stressful, but I loved it. I learned so much from other amazing and dedicated educators throughout the years. My students have also taught me so much and have inspired me endlessly.

I viewed my stepson, nieces, nephews, little cousins, and students as my children. I said quite often that I didn't want children. Then one day, when I said it-it didn't ring true anymore. So with the support of my husband, we decided to try to have a child. At a time when my stepson, nieces, nephews, and my friends' kids were all in high school or college…we had our baby boy, Arden.

Arden was healthy and such a blessing to all of us. I longed to spend as much time as I could with him, but I had to go back to teaching after a short maternity leave. This wasn't easy, but it had to be done.

At about three years old, Arden was diagnosed with autism. As a mom, worry is part of the territory. But when your child has a diagnosis-it intensifies. So, more than ever, I wanted to spend more time with Arden at home and at his school-to make sure I was his strongest and most knowledgeable advocate.

When I learned about Network Marketing-I was already with a company for a year. All I knew was that I fell in love with a product that I LOVED, and I felt everyone needed it, and I wanted to be the one to tell them! I didn't even know I could make money selling the products, but when I did-I thought this could be my ticket to spending more time with my son.

My Marketing degree was long forgotten, I was an educator! I had no idea how I was going to be able to tell others about my products. My family and friends didn't want to have anything to do with it!

The next company I joined offered marketing tools that would allow me to tell more people about my products-So awesome. However, I got something more that was unexpected: An amazing community of small business owners and entrepreneurs who welcomed me and taught me all they knew selflessly! I've learned over time that THIS is what most people are searching for and receive as Network Marketers.

I learned that as Network Marketers, personal development is crucial. Becoming a better YOU is essential and something I knew next to nothing about prior to becoming a network marketer. This was exhilarating to me. All my life, I was doing things for others, my mom, siblings, husband, child, students, and so on, and I wasn't last…I wasn't even on the list!

I hired coaches, took courses, training, read books, listened to podcasts, etc…all of which helped to make me a better marketer. An additional bonus here was that I also became a better wife, mom, and educator!

Through personal development, the Limiting Beliefs and Self-Sabotage that are a product of my childhood have diminished! I have the tools, knowledge, and routines that are making me stronger and unstoppable every day.

I have created a daily routine that sets me up for success: prayer, gratitude, meditation, exercise, healthy eating, journaling, affirmations, and vision work. I am no longer the Deneen who hides, shrinks, and remains quiet. My word for 2023 is "Serve".

I remember the days when I didn't know how to get more eyes on my products or have conversations about what I had to offer. My calling is to impact other marketers, sole business owners, and entrepreneurs by offering them the tools and knowledge they need to brand themselves properly and build a strong online presence. So, they can grow their customer base, increase their teams and scale their businesses to create the life of their dreams.

I'm so proud of my accomplishments to date: I am a founding affiliate with my company. I was honored as the top 10 in sales with the company in my first year with them. I was invited to speak and introduce company dignitaries at a corporate event. I was also honored on stage at the annual conference for an international Network Marketing coaching organization for having the highest prospecting numbers.

I am just getting started!

If you are a business owner and you are ready to scale your business, I have three tips for you:

1. Treat your business like a business, and you are its' best employee

2. Invest in yourself, Personal Development is critical for running your business effectively

3. Invest in systems and tools that for branding yourself and building a strong online presence.

About the Author

Deneen Iverson-Kidd is an American-born entrepreneur and highly-trained educator of 25 years.

She has a home business that helps other entrepreneurs and sole proprietorship owners to market their businesses easily and affordably online.

Deneen lives in Connecticut with her husband and son, whom she enjoys traveling and spending quality time with family.

Email: info@Diversonkidd.com
Facebook: www.facebook.com/deneen.iversonkidd
Instagram: www.instagram.com/deneeniversonkidd

Denny Hunt

Living the Dream

I'm Denise Hunt, although more often than not, I'm called Denny.

I've been married to Derek, a former Royal Marines Commando, for 21 years. I currently live in the wilds of Lincolnshire with my five dogs.

I've always been a proud Geordie, having been born in the back bedroom of my Nana and Granddad Donnelly's house in Newcastle upon Tyne, England. Number 1 Rutland Avenue, to be precise. Mum regaled us with the story that, although they were married, Dad slept downstairs while she slept upstairs and, although heavily pregnant with me at the time, if she wasn't up to bed in a timely manner, Granddad would be shouting down to her, "Margaretta, time for bed!"

My parents both served in the Royal Air Force. My sister, Carole and I were fortunate to travel the world with them on postings in the days when the British forces had more choice as regards military bases; Singapore, Cyprus, Australia and

Germany were some of the places we were fortunate enough to live (twice in the case of Singapore and Cyprus). But of course, in those days, international travel took longer than it does today, so we've also touched down between flights in many places, like the tiny island of Gan in the Indian Ocean, Bombay, and Calcutta (nowadays you'll recognise them as Mumbai and Kolkata). Dad was posted to the island Gan in the Indian Ocean for a 9-month unaccompanied tour, where we were all left behind in the UK. That said, Mum joined him there, and they went on holiday in Hong Kong, whilst Carole and I stayed in New Barnet, Hertfordshire, with Granddad Hayball, our paternal grandfather and his second wife, whom we called Auntie Sylvia. One of the day trips we had was to Alexandra Palace, where Granddad was surprised to learn we couldn't row, considering we'd travelled the world. I recall one of us girls quipped, "yes, but we didn't row there, Granddad." Another time we returned to their house exhausted, having wandered around central London for 11 hours. We felt like we'd 'walked our legs off'.

Moving around was challenging as a child, although we became outgoing and independent by changing school, friends, home, and country so often. It taught us to be accepting and pretty resilient from all the changes.

I recall Mum telling us that it had been tough when they were a young married couple. They would have sausages for

Christmas dinner instead of a joint of meat or a turkey. When Dad worked at the Ministry of Defence (MOD) on Whitehall, central London, he'd walk from home to his job and back again, stopping to have his homemade sandwiches in a graveyard as he enjoyed the solitude, peace and quiet.

As I write this, it's Chinese New Year 2023, the year of the Rabbit. This brought to mind when we lived in Singapore for the second time between 1968-71. One Chinese New Year, the dragon came to our home to spread good fortune. I recall vividly the dragon entering the front door and sauntering up the stairs to the two-bedroomed military dwelling we were living in, swaying back and forth, rising and falling, as the Chinese men inside danced around.

Dad was amazing to us and could turn his hand to almost anything. Nana Donnelly always kept vacuum cleaners and washing machine issues for when we would visit, much to his amusement. Or he could be found outside the front of Number 1, tinkering on his car (or someone else's), such were our visits to Daisy Hill!

He would sew us simple dresses on the sewing machine we were proud to wear. My Dad could even knit! He threw the javelin to schoolboy county standards, and I often joined him in throwing it on the field behind our house. He also played the clarinet in the bathroom of our small, terraced house in Withernsea – he said it was because the acoustics were better.

We thought it might be to stay out of Mum's way as he practiced.

I also recall the little white car we had in Singapore that we called the Flintstone's car – we had to be careful when we got in, as there were big rusty holes in the footwell – so we'd gingerly place one foot on either side of the hole. Ever apprehensive when Dad drove over puddles (especially during Monsoon season), as we'd get soaked. But it was the same car we'd be driving in, singing to the Mamas and the Papas, one of Mum's favourite bands. Happy days!

Singapore, the second time, as we called it, is where I learned to swim competitively for the Changi Marlins. This was back when Changi was a small village with a military base, although we did pass the infamous Changi Jail to get there, along with watching the aircraft cross the road as they taxied to take off. As Dad was a shift worker, we would meet him there on the grass to have a picnic and watch the planes take off and land, with pretty easy access, long before the days of terrorist threats everywhere.

I'm eternally grateful for the choices Dad made to ensure his girls had the best life he could provide.

We were teenagers living at RAF Church Fenton when we found out Mum had a chronic kidney disease. Not that we really knew what 'chronic' meant, but she was about 38, so we'd already decided that 'that was old anyway' and paid it no mind. At that time, Mum was working in a sausage factory – Porkshire (a clever bit of marketing, considering we were living in North 'Yorkshire').

But it was only once we moved to Joint Headquarters (JHQ) Rheindahlen in Germany that we fully appreciated just how poorly Mum was. Her RAF doctor in Yorkshire had told her to come to him whenever she needed to speak about the renal disease she'd been diagnosed with. Whilst she rarely did that, she could rest assured that she had the support she needed. But once we arrived in Germany and were living in the Dorthausen married quarters, assigned to an Army doctor in Ayrshire Barracks, she found out, quite bluntly, that she 'would never be cured'. That floored her for a while. It floored us all. Even the teenage daughters who thought '38 was old anyway' and who wouldn't understand for a little while what it would actually mean, living the majority of their lives without their beloved Mum.

Singlies, for those who don't know, is a term of endearment for the lads in the Forces who are unmarried, single or divorced. My Mum, or Mummy as we always called her, was one of a kind (I think most Mums are, to their children, no matter how old they get). She was so popular with our friends that we'd often find ourselves sitting in the Blue Pool restaurant and bar (later renamed The Royal, after Sarah Ferguson and Prince Andrew's wedding), surrounded by our friends, only to find they'd sloped off to sit with Mum and Dad at another table, as Mum's humour was second to none. She was simply good company. Plus, all the 'singlies' would come to our house at Christmas when they couldn't travel back to the UK for various reasons (usually they were on duty or just plain broke), and Mum didn't want them spending it on their own.

Which reminds me of a story. I've never liked turkey as a meat – I have found it too dry, personally, so Mum would always get a joint of meat comprised of lamb, beef, pork, along with a chicken instead., She was only too happy to jump up and make me a chicken sandwich whenever I might fancy one. Until one day, I followed her into the kitchen and discovered I'd been eating turkey sandwiches without realising it. How do you ever get over a betrayal like that, even in your 20's?

We were living in Germany when I finished school. My biggest ambition at that time was to be a hotel receptionist, and I knew I needed to go to a UK college to train for that. Mum never wanted either of us to leave, so I was fortunate enough to take up a clerical job in the Joint Headquarters compound, associating with thousands of multi-nationals, multi-lingual military and civilian personnel. This was an experience in itself.

I lived in Germany for almost 20 years, after school I worked in various positions, from washing pots and pans, emptying pigswill to cleaning drains in the Officer's mess and accommodation, as well as clerical jobs with the British military, and then 12 years with the US Army, namely Combat Equipment Battalion North in Moenchengladbach, running the computer department during Desert Storm; the very first Gulf war. I've slept on military cots and worked night shifts. I'm very grateful for my experiences.

Things were never the same once the Berlin Wall fell, and the US Army started reducing their military presence in Germany. By 1994 I decided it might be time to do something different, so I left my apartment fully furnished and moved to Cyprus for a few months to work. I love Cyprus to this day.

After four months in Cyprus and the weather cooling, I returned to Germany ready to pack up my things and head to the UK to start afresh. I arrived in Dover, Kent, with just my TV, sound system and clothes after my friend Diana and her son, Luis, kindly drove me over. I was fortunate enough to have the O'Brien family to help me, and after a few days with Edna and Neil, their daughter Julie and I moved into our own place. Neil was formerly in the RAF, so we had known each other in Germany. I worked a few temporary jobs (including in a factory and at a funeral directors) before getting a permanent job as a PA with Kent County Council, Adult Services.

In March 1996, I moved up to London. This was a scary move because, although I'd gone to Cyprus by myself, it wasn't as big and busy as the Capital. I worked in various temporary positions as there is always work in London if you're prepared to do most anything or have secretarial skills to fall back on. Thankfully, I was happy to do whatever, although I never had to, as office work was aplenty for conscientious, efficient and reliable people. Organisation has always been my forte, so I was very popular in many of the London offices, particularly those where I came in after another temp who just wanted to get their salary! Amongst other positions, I took on a full-time position as PA for a property investment and development company, Nightingale Estates Limited, for a few years before being made redundant. The property market was very buoyant then, and the founders/owners decided to part ways and work separately from their homes.

After that, I found myself working in Covent Garden, which was an experience, as I'd never worked in a London office before and had been allowed to wear jeans. As rules went, Covent Garden was much more relaxed than Mayfair, and the 'arty' type had offices there. I worked for an amazing man named David Warburton as his PA. But it was short-lived. He had set up the company in his bedroom – it was during the time that phone ringtones were all the trend (remember the Crazy Frog – it drove me nuts, and I know I wasn't the only one!). David was a trained musician and a very talented man. After a few months, he decided to step down as CEO and become the Executive Chairman. So, I was out of a job again – the second time in a year.

However, whilst that might sound a little dire, the situation was merely one door opening as one door closed because I found the job I have loved the most. I became an executive Office Manager for two wonderful people and stayed there for 12 years before they had to close the office and leave the UK. They were British naturalised, and their children were born here, but for various reasons I don't care to talk about here (nothing criminal or negative on their part), they chose to leave the UK. They taught me so much about a better lifestyle and treating myself well that it really opened my eyes.

It was during my time with them that I found network marketing – or maybe it found me. Neither my sister nor I had been blessed with biological children, so I always felt there must be more to life than what I had. That wasn't being ungrateful, that was simply me believing I deserved better and should seek better. I had the most fantastic job, with wonderful kind and generous people, an excellent salary, great perks and bonuses – I travelled on business. Yet I still felt there was something else for me.

I found that in my Plan B.

Have you heard of a Plan B? I think the expression gets bandied about quite a bit these days, so you may well have. Anyway, I started a little Multi-Level Marketing (MLM) business alongside my job, although I was filled with trepidation as I genuinely thought you had to go to university to learn about marketing. How wrong could I be? While MLM isn't easy all the time, it's straightforward.

I found a fantastic new community of people, who wanted me to do well, and who helped support and encourage me to be the best I could be. Something you rarely find in the job market – people are often competitive and self-involved instead. With these people, I no longer felt I was looking for anything else. Don't get me wrong, I continued to live an extraordinary life – who wouldn't live in London, earning an excellent wage and being surrounded by so many beautiful hotels selling unique cocktails and Michelin-star restaurants with celebrity chefs? But it was me who was changing. Whether I liked it or not.

I started travelling for conventions around the UK, Europe and the United States. To learn more, so I could teach and help others in their quest for a better life, for time freedom. Some even just wanted a little extra every month to treat the kids or pamper themselves or their spouses. There's no 'one size fits all'. We're all individuals, after all.

I'm pleased to say that having an online business has opened my eyes and my mind; it's made me a better person. For which I'm eternally grateful. If the lovely Leanne Davis hadn't been brave enough to approach me and ask to share information with me, I might still be laying on the couch of an evening, wondering, 'is this it?'

Since being in the online space, I've learned how to launch teams of people, I've connected with thousands, albeit a lot is on social media, so I only have to leave the house when I want to. I continue learning to empower people, especially women from all walks of life, to teach them that there is another way. It's not perfect, but it is better. I have more skillsets than ever before, and I continue my quest for self-improvement. I want my story to influence others, to help and encourage them.

I now lead a global team of amazing like-minded people with dreams and goals to fulfil, and I couldn't be prouder of how they look out for one another. We have systems set up that are duplicatable to save one another time and, more importantly, are easy to follow, learn and share

Sadly, Number 1 Rutland Avenue is no longer there, but I've come a long way since then. I know I'm where I should be. But owning investment property, being mortgage free to my detached home with a paddock for the dogs to enjoy, wearing a Rolex, turning left on the aircraft and travelling first class isn't what brings me the most joy.

My joy lies in helping vulnerable animals abused and discarded by human beings. Knowing that I can leave a legacy to help those less fortunate than me fills up my cup.

I couldn't imagine who I would be had I not had this fantastic opportunity present, but I am ever grateful that it did – along with all those that followed. But this isn't something only I can do or have done; it is available to everyone if they are willing to step forward and be brave enough to take control of their destiny.

Is that you?

About the Author

Denny Hunt is a well-rounded, well-travelled, likeable Capricorn.

She is an avid animal lover who supports various worldwide charities for vulnerable and abused animals, particularly dogs. That wasn't always her passion, though, as she didn't have the temerity or finances to support those in need.

Although no stranger to hard work or getting her hands dirty, she has excelled in the corporate world where the organisation was her forte, resulting in managing multi-national and multi-lingual support staff around the globe. Having lived in Germany for 20 years, she still has a working knowledge of the German language.

Her last job was working for high net-worth individuals in Mayfair, central London – her favourite city worldwide.

She has been married to Derek for 21 years and now lives in

rural Lincolnshire, England, with her five dogs, which affords her the luxury of running her successful social retail global business from home.

Facebook: www.facebook.com/denny.hunt.222
Instagram: www.instagram.com/i_am_denny_/

Geraldine Schollum

Be the Legacy

I sat on the plane with my one-and-a-half and 4-year-old sons, and I quietly tried to suppress my tears the entire 9-hour flight home from Hong Kong.

I didn't plan for my life to feel like I had to start all over again at age 31. But it did.

The previous ten years had been spent with my ex-husband, marrying, and moving from our hometown of Brisbane to Sydney (interstate) for his work. We both worked in corporate and enjoyed our work, but we wanted more. This would mean moving to places with more career advancement opportunities than where we were. He was very driven to climb the corporate ladder.

We decided that we would move to live and work in London. Our goal was to be able to buy our own home and pay off our house quickly.

His work asked if he would work in Edinburgh for four

months before being transferred to London. Since they offered him this opportunity, the company covered all our living expenses the entire time we lived in Edinburgh.

That four months turned into six months. We loved every minute of it.

Previously, I worked in Human Resources for a global accounting firm, and since we were only meant to be living in Edinburgh for four months, I decided I would be willing to do any work whilst I lived there. I went to a temporary job agency and landed a role working for a Fund Management company the next day.

When we were coming to the end of my ex-husband's contract in Edinburgh, my company told me that they were setting up some space in London and asked if I would help them set up a new office there. I was thrilled. I had an incredible sense of fulfilment and worthiness.

When I worked in our London office, we acquired a division of another investment bank along with 80 employees. Again, we needed a new office space, and whilst I was pregnant with my first son, I worked as my boss' right-hand woman – liaising with the builders, and design team, to create a new office space to cater for all our new staff. I worked on that project throughout the later stages of my pregnancy, often travelling between all three offices in London, working long hours. After many months of work, we finally moved all our staff into our beautiful new office. Just two weeks later, I went on maternity leave.

While I was on maternity leave with my new baby, two things happened that changed the trajectory of my life at the time.

The first, my ex-husband received a promotion at work, which meant that I did not have to return to my job financially. Since becoming a mother, I had been struggling with the thought of leaving my child in daycare five days a week. This was important to me, as my mother had been a stay-at-home mum for my siblings and me, and more importantly, we did not have any family nearby to help.

And two, the tragedy of the London bombings occurred. I was pregnant with our second child. That day, I couldn't reach my ex-husband on the phone. I could not find out anything about his whereabouts until later in the day, and he ended up walking home from his office with thousands of other people since the entire transport network had been shut down. The bombings happened nearby where we lived, and we couldn't imagine raising them in the city at the time.

My ex-husband came home from work shortly after that and stated that a colleague of his who had recently gone out to set up a new office in Hong Kong was leaving. My immediate thoughts were with the colleague, whom himself had a wife and a small toddler, wondering what they would do when my ex-husband asked me, 'what do you think about moving to Hong Kong?'…..

I said, 'sure, why not!'

Six weeks later, at 30 weeks pregnant, we were on a business class flight to Hong Kong, with a toddler and all our worldly possessions following on a boat to go and relocate to a country I had never been to, nor did I know anything at all about it.

We landed at night, and it was very hard to fully comprehend what the landscape looked like. The following day when I woke up and looked out the window, I realised it was mountainous and an incredibly bustling city. It was vastly different to what I imagined. I was exceedingly excited about the adventure ahead.

We had to set up a home from scratch for the next few months – find a new home and fully furnish it- before the second baby arrived. I was desperate to make new friends… luckily Hong Kong is the kind of place where you can make friends incredibly easily as there are so many expats living there and also looking to make new friends!

My second son was born a few months after we arrived.

We fulfilled one of our goals of buying a home back in Australia and planned to live in it eventually.

For nearly two years, we lived incredibly social, fulfilling lives.

However, it was during this time that all the changes we had been through took a toll on our marriage, and sadly our marriage ended.

I felt like my entire world had just come crashing down. I didn't even know where to call 'home'. I couldn't stay in Hong Kong. I didn't know if I could live in London; my closest family in the UK were in Ireland.

All that was left for me was to go back to Australia.

I arrived 'home' and felt so incredibly lost. I had no friendship circle. My immediate family lived a 9-hour drive north of me. My children were not yet in school, so there was no possibility of meeting and making new mum friends yet…

I felt like 'I had lost my right arm'. I was so used to asking what to do in every single situation.

And how could I possibly get full-time work as I was the full-time caregiver of the children since the boys' father had decided to stay living overseas?

Many times I felt completely lost, staring at the search bar on my computer screen, realising I could no longer search for external answers to the internal question – who am I?

"I'm just a mum".... I said to myself.

The words I dread to hear from other mothers now... I was feeling to the core of my being.

I was no longer a wife.

I was no longer a career woman – I had given that up to support my husband at the time in his career.

I was no longer a best friend to some of the most amazing women – I had left them not once, but now three times in 3 different countries in the space of 7 years.

I felt like I had no identity.

I was right back at square one. And the dark cloud that hung over me was debilitating.

Every day felt like ground-hog day.

Questions swirled through my mind. Questions about what my future would look like. I wondered, what would my future look like now?

I decided that I had to get some even thicker skin. I had convinced myself that my always optimistic personality would lead to my life someday sorting itself out.

I had faith. And I clung to my belief that life would get better.

I believed it would. There was just simply no other option.

Sometime during the first month after I arrived back in Australia, all the while, my mind was filled with fear of the unknown future, wondering how I was now going to provide for myself whilst also raising these two boys. I mentioned these thoughts to a lady I had recently met. She said, 'I think I know something that you can do...' and left it at that.

Days later, we met again, and she shared with me the concept of a home-based business I could work around my children in the hours I could commit to.

I was immediately filled with hope. This was something I felt made sense. I felt excited. My years of being a sponge for all things 'health' turned up in the form of something I could share with others and help them with. I found a passion inside me and something I could put my mind to that felt incredibly fulfilling. Knowing that an income opportunity was attached was also very exciting, as I wanted to be there for my children. I could build this business AND stay at home... or so I thought.

I continued along the journey, but more and more realised that to build the income, I would need to spend many hours away from home. This didn't feel any better than going and working in a corporate job.

Despite these challenges, I was building a solid business of extraordinary women who also wanted to impact their family's health and create income for themselves as well.

During this time, I re-married.

I didn't know at the time that the most challenging part was yet to come, and I would be tested again on a level I didn't know I could be tested to.

I continued to build my business, however, there were red flags in the new marriage that I chose to ignore.

You see, I hadn't done enough inner work to recognise what I wouldn't accept, and my optimistic self ignored the screaming that my gut was telling me something wasn't right.

Eventually, after less than two years of marriage, that marriage also failed, and I lost a substantial amount of money in a real estate decision we had made together.

I couldn't build my business successfully for years after that because I struggled with my identity and felt more lost than ever. I struggled with social anxiety. I constantly felt uneasy with anything deeper than surface-level conversations with people – I wanted to disappear.

Despite all of this, I continued to dabble in my business. I knew from my experiences how frustrating it was becoming, spinning my wheels, knowing I needed new habits because I needed REAL transformation.

I honestly had no idea where to turn. I have moved countries three times. I mean, I had survived not one but two marriage breakdowns. I had lost a vast amount of money, making poor decisions about people I thought I could trust.

Staying optimistic and praying that my life would sort itself out was only getting me so far. One day I dropped down to my knees and prayed with my entire being. I fully and completely left my life in God's hands. I could no longer pretend – inspirational quotes on my wall alone would not help me get to where I truly craved to go.

Less than a year later, I was buying my next home. Life was turning the corner.

During this time, I began to see a woman on my social media speaking about building her business entirely online, not having to leave her home, no 3-way calls, no more home parties, and no more hotel meetings. And she could teach ME how to build my business this way.

I decided to invest in coaching. It was a significant investment. I was so nervous, but in my gut, I knew I needed to invest in myself.

We started working together, and my mindset started to shift.

I knew that I needed to let go of the past to move forward, but I learned so much more about how my identity had been shaped by the beliefs that I had created from childhood.

I started to see success in this new system. I learned to brand myself on social media. I learned a duplicatable system. I was able to actively build my business AT HOME around my children......finally.

With my coach, I started working on my money mindset. Where once I felt safe and secure because I had a husband, I had to go deep into the subconscious to work on clearing away my old identity to make room for the confident new me.

Just over a year ago, I felt an incredible nudge from God to sell the home I had owned for five years. I said to myself, 'I will ONLY sell this house if I can once again become mortgage-free and buy my next home for cash'. I settled on a 'pie in the sky' amount of money that I would agree to sell the house not less than.

In a few short weeks, I had the house prepared for sale, had the property listed, and within a few days, just before Christmas last year, had several offers on the table.

After an intense and very exciting offer period, I sold my home and was able to sell and purchase my next property.

Did I receive my pie-in-the-sky amount? By God's grace, yes, and then some.

I was able to purchase my next property and contract a building team to complete a substantial renovation on the new property within 30 days – during the height of a lack of tradespeople availability.

As was always my dream, I became completely debt-free just two weeks shy of my 46th birthday.

Along the way, this journey helped me to heal. I was no longer 'just a mum', something I hated to hear other mums say.

Like a phoenix rising from the ashes, it can be a hot fiery mess.

I discovered through my experience of continuing to rise that I have a gift of connecting and being able to relate to women who have been through the valley, just like me.

I realised that my journey was to help teach me to help others. My journey was for a much greater purpose. I have always been incredibly interested in people and learning about them and their stories. What shapes people to become who they become? What stories could they tell, and what have they learned?

What if I had not persisted? What if I had given up? What if I succumbed to the dark days?

People need to know that their past is not their future. Their past is not their identity. People are not selfish for wanting more; in fact, the world is waiting for them to step up and speak up! You can create the future that you see in your mind's eye.

I am so grateful for the failures. I would not have impacted the many women I know of and others I don't know about. They have truly taught me to be who I am now.

I know that deep down inside me, I needed to believe in myself first to create the change, impact, and ripple effect I wanted to make. Many times along the way, I have had to borrow my mentor's belief in me. But I never stopped believing that I WAS meant for more.

Early on, at the beginning of this journey, I was given a book by a dear friend. It was called something to the effect of 'If things change, or you wish they would'. During my journey, I did WISH things would change. The only way for things to change is to change them yourself.

I found that I needed to create a vision for the future. A simple task I did for myself and even my children as they got older was to create a vision board. I would go to travel agents and grab their travel brochures – now we have Pinterest! I would pour through high-end magazines, cut out all the things I desired my future to look like and create something that I could look at every day. This helped to channel my focus to the things I desired in life.

Reading became something that has become a concrete part of my day. I would spend hours reading personal development each day and learning from people who have gone before me. There isn't something you are going through that hasn't already been written about by somebody else who has conquered it! Reading is critical to developing a strong mindset.

When everything seems bleak, it can feel challenging to get yourself out of like you're feeling you're in the dumps. I learned to practice gratitude. I learned to train my mind to see the good in every situation. Gratitude turns what little you have into abundance. Gratitude is so much more than saying thank you.

Gratitude changes your perspective of your world.

Finally, faith. As challenges arise, my faith only grows stronger. Learn to grow yours. If your faith is just the size of a mustard seed – it is enough to help you navigate the most significant challenges. Nothing will be impossible for you.

Through my journey, I learned to stand up and be strong. I learned to become a strong independent woman. I learned to manage my own finances. I learned to become someone I was proud of and show my boys that their mum was capable of anything we went through.

Anyone can live. But to truly live the life of your dreams requires work and dedication. The world needs that version of you that you truly desire to be.

And I want to help empower you to get there!

I want to help you learn to face life's hurdles with grit, strength, and grace.

"Our deepest fear is not that we are inadequate. Our deepest fear is that we are powerful beyond measure." — Marianne Williamson, A Return to Love: Reflections on the Principles of "A Course in Miracles."

About the Author

Geraldine Schollum is the founder of Legacy Nation, an online business that helps women over 40 create an additional income stream from their phone, on their terms.

Geraldine was born in Australia, the oldest of 3 children, to Irish immigrant parents who left everything and everyone they knew behind to create a better life for themselves. Despite her parent's sacrifice, she dropped out of college to start working. Geraldine ended up living and working all over the world for ten years before becoming a twice-divorced mother of two children.

Geraldine decided to use the despair of her situation to fuel her fire to build a new future for herself and her two young boys.

Email: geraldine@itsgeraldine.com
Facebook: www.facebook.com/geraldine.schollum
Instagram: www.instagram.com/geraldineschollum/

Jane S Tennis

It is never too late to start something today, dream a big dream, or take the first step

I just recently celebrated my 50th year as a Pharmacist in the State of Missouri (MO) in the US.

It is quite an honor and accomplishment, as many pharmacists are not able to or nor alive to reach this milestone. So, I feel pretty darn' special, that's for sure! Talking about milestones, and an extremely unique one at that, my dad and mom married in 1944 (a leap year), and following three years and seven months later, I was born. Then after another three years and seven months, my sister, Jackie, arrived, and finally, you guessed it, three years and seven months later, my young sister, Jill, came into the world. All over four leap years. We even made the St. Louis ODDITIES section in the local newspaper.

I grew up in a lower-middle-class family in Missouri and was raised with the belief that all things were possible. My family consisted of my dad, a city bus driver, and my mom, who worked from home babysitting and ironing for other families while raising us three girls.

Being a typical US family at that time, us girls played softball, and we watched a lot of free games among our family and friends who played as well.

I was the more studious one. I wanted to go into medicine. First, as a nurse and while in Washington DC at the Smithsonian Institute, I discovered I did not have the stomach for blood at all.

Instead of quitting altogether, a lady, whom I babysat for at the time, was a great friend and recommended pharmacy as an option. She knew I was good at math and science.

Thankfully, I was accepted into Pharmacy, and my mindset completely changed.

Growing up, I had many friends in sports, art, education, and gymnastics. Some of these friends, who belonged to different groups, did not get along, so to be accepted, I adopted many personalities. My high school graduation class had 1,000 in the class. This had me feeling out of sorts internally. I did not like that feeling of not being my true self.

St. Louis College of Pharmacy College 500 students total for the full five-year program. When I got accepted, I decided then and there that people would get to know the TRUE me; no more just adapting to the group that I associated with. Ironically, there were none of my other high school friends in pharmacy. So, I was totally the new kid in a new environment.

In those first 2 years, college was easy, as many of the classes at that time were like high school. But then, WOW, that 3rd year, I had to learn to study, and it was a real awakening. Several times, I wanted to quit. Except there was this one professor and his wife (Dr. and Mrs. Joe Haberle) who I really admired and still do today, even though he passed. She is one lady I still look up to. Both always seemed to know when I was down and were there to give me encouragement. I really admired and mimicked the elegance, grace, and class that Mrs. Haberle possessed, and I wanted to emulate her. My Mom was great at teaching us girls' etiquette and all; however, Mrs. Haberle elevated me to a different level of confidence.

My Dad passed my 2nd year in college, and my Mom raised us three girls alone.

I graduated in 1972 with a Bachler of Science (BS) in Pharmacy. Later, I went on to get a Master's in Business Administration (MBA) in 1998). I was not keen on retail pharmacy as most of my college work was in hospitals. I love the closeness to the patients and the ability to care for a select group of patients. So, after graduation, it was natural for me to work in a Hospital

Pharmacy. That is where I practiced most of my career. For a few years, I did Home Infusion and really loved the uniqueness and 1:1 care I could give these patients.

My career expanded into administration, and I served as a Hospital Pharmacy Director in 60-600 bed health systems. Some of these health systems had hospital and retail pharmacies, home infusion, and hospices services. I loved the hospice aspect the most! The patients, families, volunteers, staff, and physicians really embraced teamwork and looked to me for my thoughts. Sometimes, it was not drug-related, and everyone had a voice, and everyone's voice was heard.

I began my career in St. Louis, MO. I moved to Springfield, MO, where I started my administration services as a Pharmacy Supervisor; followed by moves to Kansas, Iowa, Oklahoma, Northwest Missouri, and I then returned to St. Louis in 2000. I came back to help with Jackie, as she had developed breast cancer.

My Mom needed me home (even though she had remarried) and so I moved back home to St. Louis. I was the most logical one to make this move. Jill, my younger sister, had a growing family of four children and was living in Iowa. With no children of my own, my dog and I moved back to St. Louis.

It was a rough time watching my sister as she battled cancer and lost that battle to cancer. When my Grandfather passed away in 1964, my Dad told me we were going to Kansas City for the funeral. I was told that since I was the oldest that, I should watch him closely as one day, I may need to be the stronger one. As I said, my Dad passed away in 1968. I had never cried in front of my mom or sisters. I was told to be the strong one, and I was! I believe to this day that I did as my Dad so wanted me to do and be. It was not until my Godfather passed many years later that I could cry in front of my mom.

In 2010, my mom was diagnosed with Alzheimer's. And again, I was the strong one and took care of her until we had to place her in a nursing home.

It was horrible to watch a vibrant lady deteriorate right before my eyes. Jill was still living in Alabama with her family. Just like when Jackie passed in 2001, it was me once again to be the strong one.

I made sure Mom always looked her best when I knew Jill was coming to town. In 2014, it was decided to place my Mom into Hospice care. I wanted to take my family Medical leave; however, the hospital I was working at did not like me leaving for an indefinite time frame.

My Mom was the one that I needed to be with. I could retire then and take care of her even though she was in a nursing home. That is what I did! I often wondered if my Mom knew me or not when I would be with her. However, I do remember so vividly Thanksgiving 2014. I had just finished feeding her, and I wiped her face. I must have wiped too hard, as she let out a blood-curling scream, "JANIE". I can laugh as I write this now, but I remember the embarrassment that I felt in the moment.

Mom passed away in February 2015. I was lost and did not know what I wanted to do. I was able to work most weekends and holidays as well on an as-needed basis in a psychiatric hospital. I was alone most holidays. The other pharmacists all had children at home. Hence, I would work these holidays to allow them to be with their families and children.

One year, back in my 60s, I discovered network marketing just by chance while I was reading a Facebook post. So, I sought out the lady for more information. Not long afterwards, I started a new career in affiliate marketing then moved over to Network Marketing (NWM). Ironically as that business was shut down by the Federal Trade Commission (FTC).

I met a new lady friend (Silke Carpenter from San Diego, CA) who was becoming involved with this Network Marketing business. We became great friends, and she convinced me to join her in an online home business. At one point, we were involved in 4-6 different NWM businesses. Today, we have found our home and have decided to stay with this one opportunity.

My transformation ensued...

Oh my. This opportunity had everything I was looking for and more.... way more! I found a new belief in people, discovered founders who believed in the business of supporting their people, and finally, I was in a place where I could truly be myself. In saying that, I still had much learning to do.... However, I no longer needed to look out for everyone else. This was my time to shine! I could look out for myself AND still help everyone else in my own way, not simply as others wanted me to be. I molded myself around the people I was helping.

I am learning to set boundaries.... still a little way to go. I am learning to trust myself and not rely on others.... again, still learning.

I am growing in my self-confidence. I already have self-confidence as a Pharmacist, where I care for those people who come to me for help. However, now I have to break down my inner walls, so others can get to know, like, and trust me. And with that, I am becoming more and more confident in meeting (initially) strangers to get to know them and then help them with their dreams and goals.

The biggest struggle I had in NWM was in asking these new people to invest in their future. Working in a hospital, I never had to ask for payment. It is another learning curve, but one that is becoming easier as I introduce more new people to this new opportunity.

Another strength that I am improving is that I am beginning to speak my mind more about what I want and do. It was not easy when I started, just like asking people to invest into their future, I soon realized it is about me standing by my values and boundaries. Some family members do not like this 'new me', but they're getting used to it. They are coming to the realization that I am not going back.

What does my future hold?

I love the culture my current NWM organization offers. I do not need to work solo as I work within the organization as part of a team. I can, and I seek help from other team members, those on my team, those on other teams, and I can even talk with the Executive team members, founders, and other high-level team members. I feel comfortable and grateful to seek out help from these leaders that will help me the most when I require it.

There are three great parts of this business I am loving the most!

1. TRAVEL: I have traveled to China, the Soviet Union, Mexico and have been on several cruises. These trips have enabled me to travel more. This opportunity gives me the chance to travel

the world. I get to make new friends through zooms, and I also can now visit them in their hometown. I always look forward to learning about their lives, their culture, and their country.

2. FREEDOM: I can help people reach their dreams of success and freedom, at the same time reaching my own. I am excited when I hear of their success stories, which is creating a legacy for their families and future generations. I would love to be a fly on the wall in 2050 and beyond to hear my family say, "AUNT JANE created this legacy for us to enjoy life and explore the world" through her hard work and belief in us." Others will be able to say the same to their families when they join me, and we will reach the top together!

3. As I have mentioned, I have worked in Hospice. I love the concept of helping patients and caregivers. When my MOM was diagnosed with Alzheimer's, and I watched her deteriorate before my very eyes, there was no one nor group that I could turn to and help me to understand her declining process and how I could help her the best. As a pharmacist, I understood the medications, therapy, and all that helped my mom, but there were no resources to help me (the caregiver) and my family. As a result, upon my Mom's death, and with the opportunity that NWM can provide, I have decided to create a non-profit foundation to assist the caregivers.

With the advancement of research, Alzheimer's and Dementia

patients are living 5-10-20 years with this disease. The frustrations, the worry, and life, in general, wear the caregivers out. There is NO organization that I have found to help us. I envision an organization like Hospice and Alcoholics Anonymous (AA) where the caregivers meet, talk about their issues both with the patient and with their families, express their frustrations, etc., in a non-treating environment. I believe this will help caregivers feel more positive and less confused in caring for their loved one.

Some people claim Network Marketing (NWM) is a scam. If it was a scam, please explain to me how with hard work, belief, and dedication, so many people's lives, directly and indirectly, have been changed for the positive because someone was asked to join. They saw the vision, and they acted. Most people are comfortable receiving a paycheck for a 9-5 job.

Some believe you must be a college graduate to become a success. Some people snub the beggar on the street. And we can all identify with other examples of humans with our own perspective. I ask of you, if anyone were willing to make that decision, to make a change for a brighter future, would you disengage with them.

Maybe at first, but after they succeeded, I believe you would say that you knew them when… I encourage everyone to think outside of the box, take that chance, believe, and have faith in yourself. And you, too will change, grow, and become an entirely different person. Just look at the many famous people from Colonel Sanders, Ray Kroft, Leo Iacocca, Thomas Edison, and so many more, most of whom lacked education... even the gold digger 3 feet from the gold in the mine who gave up and the next person found the fortune.

No one should be laughed at or looked down on because they believe differently. Cherish the difference in people, support peoples' dreams, and you will be surprised at what you will find. I still have lots to learn. I know I will always have lots to learn, and I never want to be afraid of wanting or seeking opportunities to learn. If we stop learning, we will die a slow and miserable death.

Remember, my friends, chin up, put a smile on your face, help your fellow humans, and you will be 100x richer in this illusion we call life. I am loving this journey. GOD BLESS each and every one of you on your journey. My future is bright! I have changed lots over these last few years. I am confident that I will not recognize myself in the coming years.

I want to reach more people and help them to learn, grow and teach others. My business will not be the same today as it will be in a year, five years, or even ten years from now. I will have accelerated my mindset, skills, confidence and grown beyond my wildest dreams. My friend circles will be in a whole new league. My family and current friends will wonder, "where is the Jane I knew". In fact, I have already been asked that very question. Do not be upset if friends leave you and new friends arrive in your sphere.

As the saying goes, not all things remain the same. Some will join for your life; and some for only a season. Accept that, and success will be at your fingertips.

About the Author

Jane Tennis lives in St. Louis, MO, where she was born and raised. She is a Network Marketer PRO. She has been a Missouri Pharmacist for over 50 years. She was the Director of Hospital Pharmacy from 60-600 bed hospitals in the Midwest; she continues to work on an as-needed basis.

She stepped into Network Marketing in her late 60's and is finding many new and wonderful information about herself and her colleagues, from mindset to time management to financial freedom. She loves to travel the world, visiting China, the Soviet Union, Mexico, on several cruises, Panama, Ecuador. There are many countries yet to visit. When not working, Jane spends time with her dog, friends, and family.

Email: RxJane@msn.com
Facebook:
www.facebook.com/profile.php?id=100081256597529
LinkedIn: www.linkedin.com/in/jane-tennis-45a44810

Janet Schoen

I grew up on a dairy farm in rural Mercer County, Ohio. This region is called the Land of the Cross-Tipped Churches due to its history and frequency of existing churches. The farm I grew up on was located on top of a hill, and on a clear day, many church steeples are visible. I am the daughter of loving parents and supportive siblings. The local communities consist of hard-working people, and I was raised to give my best efforts to all my activities.

My sophomore year in high school, I decided that my love for music and helping others was reason for me to be a Band Director. With support of my parents, I started taking French Horn lessons once a month with a professor at The Ohio State University. Mom and I made the two-hour trips together. With taking the lessons, my mom and I always made the two-hour trips together, which was always a day that I looked forward to. In hind-sight, I have grown to appreciate the time and support of my Mom during that time, for she had raised a family of six children and made time for my ambitions. The time we spent together on those trips were memorable and meant a lot to me, for it gave us time to talk and stay connected.

Unstoppable!

When my senior year in high school came, there was no searching where and what I was going to do after high school. I was headed to The Ohio State University for a degree in Music Education. I had helped younger students learn to play their instruments at our local high school, and I found that rewarding. My intentions were focused in finding an Assistant Director position at the high school level. This would also allow me to fulfill another goal of mine of having a family and being a mom someday. Having a family and having a career in music would be a dream come true for me.

Our high school band director was a graduate of The Ohio State University (OSU) and had been part of the marching band there. He was an alumnus and had dotted the "I", which is a prestigious endeavor of 'The Best Damn Band in the Land' (TBDBITL). I liked performing in the marching band in high school, so I wanted to try out for the university marching band at OSU. I had connected with other local students travelling to OSU on Tuesdays and Thursday evenings for the marching band practice. The marching band at OSU is a highly competitive environment and it is challenging to participate in. The standards for the band are high, and it takes a mental and physical commitment to earn a role in the world renown 'TBDBITL'. I was fortunate enough to make the band as an alternate my freshman year at OSU. In reflection, I suspect I was quite lucky, for on the last day of tryouts, I was doing a drill with a 360° turn move (which is literally spinning 360° on one foot) when I landed on my left ankle wrong and fell to the ground with a severely sprained ankle. I was devastated.

It turned out that I did make the band as an alternate. I was glad to be part of the band but was disappointed and ashamed I had made it as an alternate. Over time, my ankle had healed to a point that with a brace, I was able to work my way into becoming a regular and was part of TBDBILT at the Citrus Bowl that year. Following the bowl game and during the off-season, I had lost my desire to be part of the organization due to many reasons. Furthermore, I also knew that the next year in college was going to be a big growth year as a French Hornist. I was to practice multiple hours a day to prepare for moving into a year in college, where I was required to perform a solo recital.

That same year, I wasn't always focused when I practiced, and I didn't always practice multiple hours a day like I should have. We were being graded on our technical merit and performance ability to advance to the next level. My evaluation went okay but not great. When I met with my professor, he was reluctant in passing me but indicated that for some unknown reason, he felt like he should pass me and it was okay for me to proceed to the next level. This left me with a feeling of self-disappointment.

Shortly thereafter, I was head to see my cousin, who was a doctor in a nearby community, to get a medical evaluation as part of a requirement for a summer job at the OSU day care center. This day will change my life forever. I do not remember but have been told it was a hot summer day. I had asked my boyfriend to accompany me to the appointment. We didn't know at that time, but we were about to experience an event which would affect our lives and the lives of the people most dear to us forever. We were a recipient of a head-on car collision due to a young lady with a car full of other of young adults losing control of her car. She had reached back in the car to hit her boyfriend, who was pulling on her hair. At that moment, she lost control of her vehicle and crossed the grass median of a divided four-lane freeway to land her car directly in front of the car I was driving. The accident stopped traffic in all four lanes for many hours, and the accident made the local evening news. They had to use the jaws-of-life to get me out of the vehicle. My boyfriend and I were both sent to different hospitals via helicopters for emergency surgeries and medical care.

I was flown to a local hospital, where they kept me in a cold room for a few hours because they were not sure I was going to continue to live and try to stabilize me. As time passed and I was still alive, they brought me into surgery. My parents also received that dreadful phone call and, upon making it to the hospital, were informed that I may not survive and if I did, I may end up "having the mental capacity of a vegetable". Apparently, the prognosis was bleak.

Following the surgery, I remained in a coma for four days, and I experienced a closed head injury and a Traumatic Brain Injury (TBI), broken foot, and several severe lacerations, amongst other issues. While in the hospital and due to my love of music, my parents and the medical staff played music around the clock in the hopes that it would help bring me out of my coma. As a result of the accident, I woke up from the coma with the entire left side of my body paralyzed. I had lost control of the left side of my face, had difficulty swallowing and talking, could not move my left arm at will, and was not able to balance myself. Over the next several weeks, I slowly regained control of portions of my left side and started to heal. I slowly was introduced to food and had swallowing test done weekly.

When my health improved to a point where I was released from the hospital, I was to go to a inpatient rehabilitation hospital. I was only twenty years old and could not walk, had trouble speaking, was having double vision, and could not feed myself. Due to the severity of my injuries, my parents weren't given many options to choose from for adequate rehabilitation venues. Fortunately, located in Columbus, Ohio, was Dodd Hall, a part of The Ohio State University Medical Center.

When I was transferred to Dodd Hall, I was sleeping most of my days still, and my mom wondered how I would even be able to be a part of the therapy and receive the services. The doctor reassured her it was important to get me moved as soon as possible.

The day they transferred me to Dodd Hall the nurses gave me my first shower since the accident. I remember it well, for I was put in a shower chair, which is a seat similar to a toilet seat. They washed my body and hair. I remember thinking I know what they are doing, but I am not capable of doing it. I was paralyzed on my left side and had a tube in my stomach that was used to feed me due to my throat having paralysis still. I was never so humiliated in my life.

After the shower, I sat in my room and prayed. I remember thinking, "Jesus, I am only 20 years old, and it is not ok for me to be like this. I am to get my college degree, get married, and have a family with children." It is at that time I had decided that if I could just be able to do one 'new' thing each day, I would be able to make those dreams happen. It was a long 7 weeks, but I left Dodd Hall walking, still with double vision, able to feed myself, and moving my left side.

The first phase of recovery was done, and the dreams were still in progress. I then did additional time of outpatient rehabilitation at Miami Valley Hospital in Dayton, OH, three days a week. At this time, I was back living with my parents in Mercer County, and my mom and older sister took turns driving me to therapy. This continued for three months, and my dream of going to college, to finish my music degree, and a family was still at the forefront of my thoughts.

I returned to college after Christmas, little over 6 months after the accident, only to be faced with many new obstacles. I was now a disabled student at a huge university in the coldest time of the year. I had to relearn many skills, like taking notes, how to play the French Horn again, and test-taking skills. I was still experiencing double vision, so my textbooks had to be put on tape for the visually impaired students and was usually not available until late in the college quarter, making studying that more challenging. With a whole bunch of determination, prayer, and persistence, I gave a solo French Horn recital, and I graduated with my Bachelor of Music Education without a certification. I was so happy and grateful to have accomplished my first dream. It was also at this time I got engaged to be married to my boyfriend, who was the same person that experienced the accident with me. We were married a little over four years after the accident.

After the wedding and now that college was completed, I found myself with a dilemma. I didn't have anything to wake up to every day. I was experiencing residual pain in my right foot, post traumatic headaches, and was battling with self-worth issues. I worked a few temporary jobs to only find the physical pain in my foot and my inability to adapt to the work environment in a timely manner very frustrating and feeding my challenges with self-worth and wanting to earning an income.

We started having a family in 2000. We had three boys that have grown to three young men that are my pride and joy. We are proud to have them as our children, and these young men have helped me as much as I hope to have helped them. They are now starting their journey with adulthood, and I now find that I have interest in joining the workforce outside of the home. This brought back all the feelings of unworthiness, pain, frustration, and self-sabotaging I had prior to having children. After having a few jobs which did not turn out to be a fit for me, I decided to start a home travel business. Although this was something new for me, I had tried various part-time home sale endeavors while raising our children with little success. This time around, I felt as though I understood the business details better. This new journey of mine was not going to be easy, but I was able to be home for the remaining years that my boys are still living with us and with my husband more.

After finding some success and seeing that true success had to come from the inside out. The problem I was confronted with was I didn't have an understanding on how to find it within me, so I started receiving Mindset Coaching. At first, I had trouble with understanding the message behind the coaching, but as I came to learn, ego is not just someone thinking higher of themselves, and later being introduced to the concept of finding presence. After a year of having monthly calls, I looked into receiving more coaching. I had a coach that really resonated with me and my spirituality. After a month of weekly coaching, I had made a comment to another coach that I thought that being a coach would be so fulfilling and seemed like something that would fill my heart. With encouragement, I joined their coaching certification program. I have found that with continued learning and by implementing self-presence has changed my life. After all the therapy I had done after the accident, I realized that I had been living my life with many habits, some of which were not productive to self-growth. As many people may know, we all have habits that serve us and habits that don't help us be, do, and have more in life. When I started checking in with myself and becoming aware of self-presence, I was able to do everyday things that I struggled with for years in changing, I am now making progress with those changes. I also have learned that our emotions are just that, emotions. They are neither good nor bad. When I am self-present, it allows me to make a choice about how I want to feel and do. This has helped me to process my feelings about the loss of my parents and a life that was taken away from me at the age of 20.

I now have my coaching certification for helping individuals with their grieving process. With my life's journey I can be empathetic and understanding to how people feel about their life situations. I continue to grow my mindset along with my coaching abilities and look forward to helping people understand their soul is made in the same love as the love that created them. Helping people find confidence, motivation, and being a service to others is what truly drives my heart, and I understand that when my eyes open in the morning to a new day, it is a gift. I am here to make a difference in someone's life, and I have a job to do.

Here are the steps to the system that I used to overcome great odds in life. I used a system which I learned in my coaching certification course: The Law of Attraction (Law of Love). At the time I used these steps, I did not have the knowledge, and now realize it was a gift that was given to me to achieve my goals in life.

The first step is getting crystal clear on beliefs that don't serve your life for good. The second step is getting crystal clear on which beliefs you want to promote to serve you. Then, identify the unwanted beliefs, acknowledging their presence, and cast them away. The fourth step is to promote the positive belief you wish to obtain and take the necessary action to apply it to your life. The final step is surrendering or letting go of how or when the change in beliefs occur. It is important you do the necessary work and trust that it will work out. Usually, things will appear in a better way than you expect them to occur.

These steps are applicable to all parts of our lives, whether it be your physical, mental, career, or spiritual beliefs, which will help you achieve more in your life. This, in turn will allow you to help others do the same in their lives.

About the Author

Janet Schoen is married and is a mother of three young men. She has been a stay-at-home mother for twenty-two of her 25 years of marriage and is a trauma survivor. Since her trauma, she has struggled with the idea of finding her place in the world and understanding how to 'fit in' while dealing with the effects of the trauma. She understands that her story of survival can be helpful for others, and her deep desire in wanting to help other trauma survivors, and their families, is a driving factor in wanting to share her story. Through her journey, she has achieved coaching certification and looks forward in helping others to have more joy, love, peace, and fulfillment in their lives. Janet also aspires of meeting new people and becoming a motivational speaker.

Facebook: www.facebook.com/janet.schoen.9
Instagram: www.instagram.com/janet_m_schoen/
Website: www.janetschoen.com

Kate Trevean

I'm writing this chapter not for myself but in the hope that by sharing, I might help inspire other women that read my story. That someone might end this chapter believing a little more in themselves, dreaming bigger, or even just finding comfort that they are not alone in their challenges during this journey of life.

I'm not going to share any huge trauma and my incredible recovery or a childhood filled with danger or tragedy, but as I have grown my knowledge on my journey to develop, I now recognise that we all have our story.

Even with a relatively balanced upbringing, we all experience significant life events from childhood into adulthood. Even if we look back now and see an event that happened wasn't anything, we would currently be affected by, at that moment, that life event had an impact. It creates an emotion and a story that we then carry with us, contributing to how we perceive ourselves and the world. Our behaviours, personality, beliefs, and so much more are created and built over time and depending on how we choose to evolve, we carry certain parts with us into our future. Many of these can be positive, and other parts not so much.

I'm coming to you as an everyday woman, a mother, a businesswoman, someone who has definitely faced many challenges in life (as we all do) and has chosen to focus on aiming to be the best version of myself, to work to build a life that I love and to not settle with just being the past version of myself.

Sometimes it can feel as though it's difficult sharing the story of "success" without the beginning being at absolute rock bottom, but my aim is to help you with that by sharing my version of success, assisting you to identify what yours is and helping you understand that this looks different to everyone.

I had what most would call a relatively normal upbringing. My parents were divorced when I was very young. I don't actually have any memory of them being together. I would say we were middle class, I never went without, but I wouldn't say we had noticeably excessive finances. There were definitely many limitations. Everything I have now is due to hard work and my own efforts. I had my first job at 14, purchased my first car myself at 18 (it was brand new) and continued to build finances from there. I have always loved numbers and, through my own self education, learnt to budget and manage finances. I had a few examples of loved ones with great success in life, where it was later lost. This has definitely been an underlying fear of mine, but a story that I am here to rewrite.

Growing up, I was never really someone that felt like anyone. I lacked self-confidence, compared myself to others and never identified myself as feeling good enough for much. As a child, I was shy and, even in my mid 20,'s would go bright red when any attention was on me. Due to being so unsure of myself, I never really decided on a career direction and went straight into the workplace from school. My jobs have very much been in service and support roles. I have always loved helping others in some way and thrived in the workplace when I could go above and beyond what was expected. I'm not someone who really enjoys the spotlight, but I do definitely like to be assured that I'm doing a great job. I have always been quite maternal, loved babies, and from a young age, I looked forward to being a mum.

When our first son was born, I had the first taste of being a woman with the mental battle of not earning an income and the crazy world of being a new mum. I remember the internal talk of absolutely loving being home with my baby but also feeling so unsure in my value or where I was headed!. I returned to work part-time when our little man was eight months old, my more mature self now sees this wasn't just a financial thing but also me feeling lost in myself and not feeling like I was enough without the external validation as a well-performing employee.

Business life...

Just after our second child was born, I discovered my 'accidental career' in network marketing. I say accidental because I was on maternity leave from my job, and initially, I just wanted to try the products, little did I know that was just the beginning. So in 2014, with a newborn and a two-year-old, my business began. I followed the little niggles, not knowing where it would or could lead. For me as an individual, this business actually didn't make too much sense, but there was just something inside of me that kept telling me to do the next thing, to not give up when it got hard but try it for one more week - I mean I loved skincare and makeup. Still, I didn't wear lipstick which was/is one of our stand-out products. I definitely wasn't someone keen to be in front of a camera. I would be so embarrassed demonstrating products for people, and I was far from keen to face the discomfort of the stigma attached to the industry.

Isn't it funny how that one decision we make can actually change our lives? For me, this was definitely one of those moments. I was a tired mother with a newborn and toddler who wanted to buy a lipstick even though I didn't even wear lipstick. Have you had those moments in life when you look back, it really changed so much for you?

So it began. I tried the products, I sold products and then built an incredible team who, in that next year, went on to be the first in the country to sell over USD 1 million. It actually ended up being over USD 3 million and has been well over that every year since. I have earned car payments and trips to incredible destinations, which I will be forever grateful for. I have so many phenomenal women in my life who were once strangers and are now beautiful friends. The financial freedom and time freedom with a young family has been such a huge blessing - Earning an income from home while being able to be present with my young children and work my business around them is something I appreciate so much, oh yes it was a crazy juggle (especially when it was three kids aged five and under) but time really does fly, and my mumma heart really loved this part.

That gives you an overview of my journey and is definitely not to big note myself. All of these achievements are absolutely a team effort, results that take many incredible people coming together, sharing their strengths, growing and learning together. Trust me, I am far from being the strongest leader in this pack, but this shows how when women come together with our knowledge, strengths and experience, we really can achieve incredible things. I have seen it, and I have been a part of it. We lift each other up rather than competing and know that there really is enough for everyone. We are all just as deserving as the other.

Since being in my business, I have developed a love for

personal growth and development. I have invested a lot financially into furthering my knowledge through courses, events, conferences, coaching and certifications. This interest initially began when I really had to start doing the work for myself to expand both personally and professionally. When you have had low self-esteem, negative self-talk and lacked confidence for a large portion of your life, it's going to take work to re-frame and make changes. It takes stepping into discomfort and really getting honest with yourself.

We are all on our own journey in life and see things through our own lens. That lens comprises events from childhood, our upbringing, culture, life events, exposure to external factors like media, teachers and coaches. This can also change and evolve as we learn, grow and do the internal work. Just because we have lived or seen things a certain way for a really long time, it doesn't mean we have to stay stuck there and cannot change. In fact, two people can be living under the same roof side by side but seeing things very differently, one abundantly grateful and the other in a scarcity victim mindset. The reality is that no one else can save us but ourselves. No matter how much others around us can try and lift us up, they can only do so much. We need to make a commitment and a decision. It gets to a point where you get sick of your own excuses and tired of not reaching the heights you know you can, not just in business, but in life, in health and in every other area you know you were made for more and need to stop settling.

In my experience, there is a common thread that comes up for many women, usually along the lines of self-sabotage, lack of confidence and low self-worth. These are all challenges I have faced myself, and now enjoy helping other women work through them. These blocks can come up in various ways and be presented differently for each individual. What can appear to look like a specific challenge on the surface usually comes from a deep underlying story that is linked to one of these areas. As women, we can be very hard on ourselves. We juggle so much, which means we can, at times we, also lose ourselves. We go through so many different seasons in life, each with new challenges. I am now learning, especially as my children grow, that the journey is truly never-ending, not just as a female in life and in business but as a mother. It feels like every stage faces new levels of excitement that is also matched with another part of sadness where we are letting go of what was. No matter which area we look at, it's quite comparable. Just when you feel like you have it all figured out, a new level of challenge arrives, discomfort of the unknown with new challenges to be faced. This is not something to be feared, and often through our greatest challenges come our greatest breakthroughs - life is a balance of both light and dark, where we can choose to embrace the polarity, understanding that it is all a part of the human experience.

Three major areas of impact...

Getting uncomfortable - feeling the fear and doing it anyway.

This has been absolutely HUGE for me! I had never felt confident in myself and always worried about what others would think, so I really had to embrace stepping into discomfort. Running a business and showing up as a leader meant that there was a lot of growing to do, and there will continue to be (for eternity). Perception is everything, and we are so great at getting in our own way - I have examples where someone has told me how great I was and how it was so easy for me when on the inside, I was actually beating myself up for being so bad, and my stomach was doing flips from nervousness!

My biggest tip is to focus on the small steps and to take them. We are so fearful of getting it wrong, but really it's mainly the thoughts in our own heads telling us what it 'should' look like. We compare our day one to some else's day one thousand, expecting perfection when in reality, perfect doesn't actually exist.

Did you know that fear and excitement actually feel the same in our bodies? It's our brain providing the thoughts attached to give it that meaning? Next time you feel that discomfort reframe your thoughts and tell yourself just how excited you are.

Working outside of your comfort zone is just like building a muscle. This means that over time you will gain strength and confidence, that thing that you were once fearful of will become your new comfort zone. Each small step compounds over time, and sometimes the result in return isn't instant but know and trust that it is coming. "You don't have to be great to start, but you have to start to be great" ~ Zig Ziglar

The bad news- the next new level has a new level of discomfort to break through, even those you think have their challenges. The challenges might look different to yours, but that at every level, something new will come up.

The good news - you are already stronger, more confident, more advanced, have tools to lean on and are reaching levels you once thought weren't possible. Yay!

I have many times convinced myself that I'm ok with settling, that I'll let go of looking to grow and stay comfortable, but the reality is we as humans thrive off growth and staying comfortable really doesn't feel that great, especially when you feel like you are made to do so much more. Sitting still almost feels like going backwards, especially if the world and people around you are moving forward.

A great resource if you feel like you need some extra help - The 5 Second Rule by Mel Robbins

Action and learning

We are in a world with so much information at our fingertips. What a privilege that is. If you want to learn something, you can so easily tap into a course, free information online or get multiple books from experts who have spent years educating themselves. The one challenge I see with this is the risk of overconsumption, don't get me wrong, I don't think we ever stop learning, but I do know that we can easily get stuck in the learning and not the doing. In business, this can be a challenge because it feels like we are spending so much time and effort, but the fact is we aren't actually taking the actions to move us forward. The true learning is in the doing, having a balance of growing knowledge but then putting it into action. I like to use the example of swimming lessons or riding a bike - we could sit and watch, read about it, write notes which would all be amazing, but until we jump in that water and ride that bike, how much further can we actually progress? The ACTION is needed.

Choice and decision

Every day when we wake up, we get to choose who we show up as that day. We get to choose our thoughts and what we focus on. Life isn't perfect for any person walking this earth, but if we are waking up, then there is always something to be grateful for.

Some days choosing to show up as the best version of yourself feels easy and powerful, it flows, and the day is incredible. Other days it doesn't come quite as easily. We feel flat and challenged in all areas. Know that no individual is immune to this. The ebbs and flows of life are just that. It's how we choose to deal with it all that makes the biggest difference.

An awesome re-frame that I absolutely love is instead of saying or thinking, "I have to", flip that to "I get to". This give a whole new perspective to parts of our life that might feel mundane or tedious. Quite often, we can slip into default mode and really need to get back to our conscious present thoughts and realise that in life, quite often, the little moments are actually big moments. They are things that we once wished for, and now that they have arrived, we are searching for something else. Really choose to be present, be grateful and enjoy the journey. Happiness is a choice, looking to grow is a choice, investing in yourself is a choice, making your health a priority is a choice. What choices are you making? Are you living in default mode, or are you deciding and intentionally choosing?

We can make a decision at any time to make a change, it doesn't have to be a new year, on Monday, or when "this" happens, then I'll do it. In any moment, the choice is yours!

My vision for the future...

As I approach turning 40 in around 12 months' time I am aiming to be the best version of myself in all areas in health, happiness, love, life, business and wealth. I aim to continue to build a life by design and help other women do the same. I'm all about loving people where they are at and understand that we all have different versions of what success looks like. Just because I might want a certain income or lifestyle, that does not mean it's the same for all. I will continue working with women in the areas of motivation and mindset, supporting them to break through self-sabotage to feel empowered to reach their full potential. I am moving into a new season with all of our children now at school, which means new levels to reach for myself both personally and professionally.

My children are my absolute world, and I feel so blessed to have been chosen to be their mama. They are my why, and the life I aim to build is for them. I do not aim to leave a financial legacy but of love, connection, beautiful memories, contribution, knowledge, learnings, and so much more.

Lastly, your reminder. Give yourself grace. You are deserving, you are powerful, and you can do great things!

Kate xx

About the Author

Kate is a 39-year-old, Melbourne (Australia) based mum of 3.

A self-confessed introvert obsessed with creating a life beyond mediocre with the belief that we truly can be, do and have it all. Kate is a multiple 6 figure p/a earner through her network marketing business, which is about helping women become the best version of themselves, both inside and out. Kate thrives off seeing other women succeed in life and in business, knowing the power of aligned expansion and empowered evolution.

Instagram: www.instgram.com/kate_trevean
Facebook: www.facebook.com/kate.trevean
Email: katetrevean@outlook.com

Kellie Zentz

My life up to this point has essentially been a series of accidental blessings, and I wouldn't change not even one moment of it.

I am sitting down to write my story as I reflect on all that occurred in 2022 and look ahead to all that is to come in 2023 and beyond. This is only one chapter, so you will only receive the highlights. I hope you are inspired by the following events that led me to achieving financial freedom at age 35. I intend to share with you all my accidents that have proven to be accomplishments through lessons learned so that you can either embrace your own accidents or be encouraged to live your life with purpose early on—simply depending on where you are currently at in your own chapter. Keep in mind that my accidental blessings do not necessarily preclude any person from still following a similar path. Instead, I highlight them to show that if I can achieve financial freedom at an early age, then truly any person can. My story is not full of a series of spectacular events, but rather a series of normal everyday happenings, and even some setbacks, that I chose to make the most out of in order to maximize the benefit and continue progressing forward.

Let's start from the beginning. The beginning of my adulthood years, that is. I can fast forward through my childhood in summary by telling you that I did not grow up surrounded by wealth. The opposite is, in fact, true. I did grow up surrounded by much love, and I believe that to be just as important. I mention the lack of wealth to also tie in the fact that I grew up with zero ambition for education or stellar achievement, and that is why my first accidental blessing was going to college. It was a stereotypical story in which I followed a boy spontaneously, without my own clear path. To say that my mom thought I was a bit nutty for believing I would go to college is an understatement, and not because she felt that I would fail... in fact, my grades were always excellent. She had no idea how I would afford such an endeavor. But through the mentorship and guidance of that boyfriend's father, I was able to navigate through college applications and financial aid assistance. That is how I ended up in an undergraduate program studying pharmaceutical science setting the stage for a future career and the beginning of establishing my goals of success.

Let's fast forward to my third year of undergraduate studies. The boy is out of the picture at this point, and I am about to learn what my second accidental blessing in my series of life events is. I fully believed that studying to be a pharmacist required only completing the four-year degree program I was in. In that third year of studies, I learned I needed to sit for an entrance exam into pharmacy school and had more applications to fill out. I learned that a pharmacist completes their four-year undergraduate program and then applies for a four-year Doctor of Pharmacy program.

Having already been taking out student loans, only to discover that the bachelor's degree I was close to completing would earn me zero income at that time (or even at this time, for that matter) was a bit overwhelming. While my second accidental blessing of not thoroughly examining the education requirements to pursue my chosen career was a bit overwhelming, it led me to apply and get into an excellent pharmacy school. It also certainly shuffled around my next ten-year plan quite a bit...

Fast forwarding a bit more. I was in my third year of my Doctor of Pharmacy program. I was at a pharmacy conference far from home, surrounded by some of the best friends I would ever have. At this point, I decided to sign up with a retail pharmacy chain as my chosen career path after graduation. However, I had friends who were still deciding between applying for residencies for hospital pharmacy positions, going the retail pharmacy path, or even seeking other opportunities. I was mindlessly browsing career booths while they were intently seeking out conversations with potential future employers.

This is where my third accidental blessing occurs.

A military recruiter saw an opportunity to start a conversation with the mindless wanderer that was me and gave me the full-on pitch for why a career in the military is the absolute best decision ever to make. He was very convincing, mainly when he spoke on student loan repayment benefits. I was a hook, line, and sinker.

Speeding ahead just a little bit further this time... I was commissioned as a Captain in the United States Air Force. My fourth accidental blessing was not correctly knowing how to inactivate an intrusion alarm in the pharmacy, which led me to meet the man who is now my husband, a Security Forces Officer. That's an entire story for another time.

I had come from a background of being raised by a single mama who loved with a passion but struggled daily to make ends meet. This drove me to pursue a career and a middle-class income that most would be content with. I was undoubtedly pleased; at this point, I was married to an accomplished man who was also an officer in the Air Force. We earned a comfortable income, had a ton of stability, and had just bought our first home together. This is the year 2013, and life was good. So good that I had accomplished all my set goals up to this point in time, so it was time to make some new ones. This is how I became interested in real estate.

I want to take a pause for just a moment to say that up until this point, my path has relied heavily on completing a graduate-level degree. While this path worked tremendously well for me to begin my growth in wealth, I will say that it is not even slightly necessary. I personally do not regret my background in acquiring an education because I believe it built necessary confidence and the ability to advance my critical thinking skills that I did not innately learn while growing up. A formal education pushed me outside of my comfort zone and exposed me to much of the world that I would not have seen through my small-town living. And it did not hurt that my education led to receiving an initial comfortable living. In moments of reflection, though, I do believe there are many paths that can be taken to achieve all the same, including taking some time to travel or learning a trade that requires less time but also is profitable.

Back now to my new interest in real estate and setting new goals..

Buying our first home was much easier than I had anticipated, and we were making more money than we needed to live off. So, my first goal was to plan to increase our real estate portfolio. We planned to live off one paycheck and invest the second. This allowed us to pay off our first home within five years, and then we bought a second home, a third home, a fourth home, a fifth home, and finally, a sixth home. In the military, it isn't uncommon for Officers to move every couple of years, so with each move, we purchased a home and rented it when we moved. That is how we now have six rental properties, the last being an Airbnb multi-unit home that we absolutely adore.

Our second goal was to pay off our student loan debt within ten years. We both were essentially walking mortgages. For my husband, we made a game plan to pay his down with our earned income. For myself, the military had a loan repayment program and a retention pay program for Officers with professional degrees. I opted to take the retention pay instead of the loan repayment with the plan to stay in the military for ten years. You see… at the time of writing this; the government offered an incentive to pay off remaining student loan debt after ten years of serving in a public service position. So, I committed myself for ten years, and we used the retention pay to invest in the real estate we were purchasing along the way. This was a sacrifice that has more than paid itself off.

Finally, our third goal at the time was to be proactive in promoting medical mission trips. I had a true passion for using my clinical knowledge in the mission field while at the same time sharing the love of Christ. This passion led me to my first experience with network marketing. My fifth accidental blessing of starting a nonprofit fundraising platform for medical missions and so many other wonderful causes. The first network marketing platform I joined was simply one that I loved the products of, and I joined intending to host "parties" for friends who were going on mission trips and donating my commissions earned toward their trips.

What was meant to be a small fundraising platform for close friends quickly evolved into a booming fundraising platform that branched far outside of medical mission trips. I promptly had youth sports teams, advocates for animal rescues, families wanting to fundraise for personal medical causes, etc., reaching out to seek assistance with setting up events. The platform boomed within the first year of originating to donating over $100,000 annually to many different causes. With the growth, we also added fellow consultants from various product lines to join in on the fun, exposing me even more to network marketing platforms.

I am going to fast-forward one last time to the current day. We are wrapping up the year 2022. I will be exiting my Air Force career in just a couple of months, which caused me to begin thinking about future goals again. My passion has evolved from medicine to network marketing and real estate. My excitement has been sparked by the thought of working outside four walls on my own time. My desire has evolved from achieving comfort to exceeding my wildest dreams.

Six months ago, I decided to hire a business coach to coach me through the strategy of capitalizing on the network marketing opportunity. Up until this point in my life, I have had a mother that has guided me through how to survive in this world, a pastor that has led me through my spiritual journey, a husband who has been committed to our journey together, a nutritionist that has educated me on proper eating and exercise to meet my fitness goals, and mentors both in and outside of work that have coached me throughout my career on decision making and avenues to pursue. I find it so fascinating that most entrepreneurs, based on my experience thus far, do not invest in a business coach but rather stumble through the process of building an online presence, platform, and business without much guidance. I recognize that I have been led along the way by a coach or mentor who has gained some life experience in whatever it is I am aiming to pursue. Therefore, I hired a business coach, and with her coaching and my being coachable, I earned a huge bonus that my chosen company pushed out within my first three months of being onboard. I surpassed my goal set for sales to bring in or team members to sign on, all with strategies I would not have known to use.

I am at the point of having financial freedom at the age of 35. I don't say that to brag but rather to remind myself. The blessing behind the disbelief of that statement is that it is indeed a fact, so I now know that my wildest dreams can be a reality. I have proven this to myself. Transitioning out of the military had at one time always meant that I would move into a retail pharmacy position. However, real estate and network marketing have become my passion. Both also exist outside of four walls and allow me to create my own schedule and be the master of my own time. I believe both will excel me forward to turn my wildest dreams into a reality.

In my first six months of network marketing, I brought home a paycheck nearly equivalent to my salary earned as a pharmacist! If you don't recall, I spent eight years studying for the position to make that salary as a pharmacist. That is simply mind-numbing, in my opinion. To top it off – I LOVE my network marketing position. Do not get me wrong, I love serving patients on the mission field, but corporate pharmacy is not the most fulfilling role, in my opinion. In network marketing, I get to build relationships with my customers; I can fulfill the needs that they may have to increase their confidence and help them live their best version of themselves. I can bring on new team members and walk them through the process of achieving their goals and fulfilling their ambitions. I can work with women worldwide to achieve a level of financial freedom without going down the same path I did regarding earning a college degree and sitting for licensing exams. Or even to share the opportunity with fellow professionals who may simply desire the same time freedom that I do. I find so much fulfillment in the whole line of work, and in my first six months, I earned a nearly equivalent paycheck to the one I am walking away from.

I am going to describe to you my wildest dreams at this stage of my life. My dreams will certainly become a reality because that is the track record I have built for myself. If not through my diligence, they will be achieved through another series of accidental blessings.

My wildest dreams consist of me achieving my first million-dollar year and building a team of hundreds of women over the next five years. And several of them will also be on their way to doing the same. I dream of building our real estate portfolio 10-fold into 100 doors in the next ten years. My dream is to continue to grow our nonprofit platform and give back at least $500,000 annually worldwide.

These dreams will become a reality. I believe that we must all dream bigger than our minds can accept. That a dream too small or too realistic is an insult to the God you follow. I encourage you not to box yourself in. If you are beginning to realize your dreams, learn from my accidental blessings and go into your goals set with more intention and strategy. If you have experienced your own random blessings, I encourage you to learn from them and share them just as I have shared mine.

If I could summarize anything I would do differently, it would be to invest more boldly in real estate and dream more audaciously than I did at the beginning. Less risk leads to less reward. It's true in the stock market, and it's true in life. I wish to dream daringly and with braveness, to set my personal and professional goals extended far out of reach to prove to myself repeatedly that I can make myself uncomfortable and overcome any challenge—first, the challenge, and then the change.

My end-state goals have always encompassed leaving the world a better place than I found it.

To not just positively impact one person but to impact hundreds of people positively. To teach others that we all have a purpose and unique gifts and are all meant to do great things.

To encourage others to step outside of their comfort zone and experience the world. Lastly, I want to see women embrace their gifts, take control of their circumstances, and change the world one accomplished goal after another.

Thank you for being a part of my story.

About the Author

Kellie Zentz is a network marketing entrepreneur, a real estate investor, a best-selling author, the Founder of Spread the Love Fundraising, and a licensed pharmacist.

At the completion of 2022, Kellie achieved a level of financial freedom at the age of 35 that is allowing her to continue pursuing her passions she desires. Her ultimate desire is to mentor other women on how they can realize their full potential and do the same.

Kellie currently lives in Rhode Island with her husband and two fur-baby kitties.

She also has a passion for traveling, and with her husband being an Active Duty Air Force Officer, she lives a life of moving around frequently and is always exploring the world.

Facebook: www.facebook.com/kelzentz
Instagram: @KelZentz
Email: worldwidelove00@gmail.com

Leanne Makinson

From the outside looking in...

When you look at my family from the outside looking in, it didn't look that different from any other standard family of four. My mum, dad, younger brother, and I spent Saturday nights in front of the TV with a family picnic watching entertainment TV. We went on standard two-week holidays to Europe and sat around a pool, but when I got to around the age of ten are when my first memories started of the fights, the arguing, the drinking, and a massive elephant in the room that we very rarely talked about..... my dad.

One of the first times I remember my dad having an episode was on a Saturday. He'd done his usual party trick and started drinking high-strength beer at 10.30 in the morning, then proceeded to start an argument with my mum until the argument got so bad that he threw her out of the house and locked her out. I waited for a moment until he was out of site, unlocked the door and ran after her dragging her back down the street to the house in my pyjamas. I just felt so ashamed that this was happening, and I felt so deeply sorry for my mum.

We were never a family that really talked, and I just thought that was normal, but the more time I spent with my friend's parents, the more I realised my family dynamic was way off where it needed to be. We rarely talked about the events that happened with my dad and the abuse (both physically and mentally), and everything would keep getting swept under an imaginary carpet for years. What baffles me is that neither parent has ever questioned why both their kids were in counselling and therapy, or maybe they did, but in true Makinson style, it was just never talked about.

My relationship with my mum is such a bitter pill to swallow. It's the relationship I desperately wanted but was always far out of reach. I watched her become so controlled by my dad that she lost herself in him. She lost all her friends due to his behaviour at parties and social events, even my mum's parents didn't have much respect for my dad either, as he was caught dating other women at the same time as my mum at the beginning of their relationship. She lost her self-worth and her beautiful personality; he did dim the fuck out of her light.

It wasn't until the back end of 2022, after a call with one of my mentors, that we had a breakthrough. I uncovered that the reason I have control issues was due to me not being able to protect my mum growing up – I carried this for over 20 years, and it had a massive effect on so many parts of my life, but now that I look back on it, it makes complete sense.

There was something always missing in my childhood, and it's only until recently that I've realised this, but there was never any acknowledgement, praise, or support in my family dynamic. There was never an 'I'm so proud of you' or a 'well done, you did great!' It just never happened. Mum came to plays, recitals and parents' evenings, but my dad? Never once, not to anything. His excuse would be down to him working away for work, which he often did, but I do always wonder whether he worked away so much as it was the easier option for him. I'll never know this, but the thought has crossed my mind a lot growing up, especially when he would be in the pub on a Friday night after working away for weeks instead of being at home with his family.

I've done a lot of work on forgiving my dad, the events that are now in the past and the version of him that tainted my childhood so severely. I hung on to the resentment for many years. It became my story, and the pain of it led to me making so many bad decisions. We have a better relationship these days, and I see him regularly. I know my dad carries the burden of the past and that he'll never be able to change it.

My acting out started when I hit high school. I used to think my acting out was down to a change in environment, hormones and falling in with a wrong crowd, but the reality is that having an absent mum and dad had everything to do with this.

Years of feeling rejected and abandoned were finally growing into a big, fat ugly head.

It started with smoking cigarettes at the age of 11 and then progressed to cannabis when I was 12. I got involved with some unsavoury characters, but I didn't care. I was finally getting attention. The attention I'd been craving for so long from my parents had finally come along but in some very dangerous, unpredictable ways. To this day, I honestly think I could have died with some of the situations I put myself in. Getting blackout drunk at such an early age, hanging about with people I hardly knew and putting myself in the centre of some wildly fucked up situations makes me so sad for this girl that just wanted to be loved. She didn't know any different, and she was so young and naïve.

From the age of 13, saw me progressed to more potent substances like ecstasy and cocaine. I was officially a raver, and misbehaver caught up in the 90s rave scene, and it was the perfect place to numb and suppress any pain or emotions I had been feeling. It was the escape I was looking for, but it led me to even darker places. I embarked on a journey of stealing, getting wasted regularly, binge eating, completely rebelling against my mum and dad, and failing at school.

I was 19 when I fell into recruitment and didn't even know what recruitment was until I started working in the industry! I started working for a small, family-run recruitment agency, but this was short-lived, and it only lasted for a year until the business closed. I had a taste for something I immensely enjoyed, the money was good, and the job wasn't rocket science, so I quickly found another role. I bounced around a few recruitment firms after this; as much as I loved recruitment, a significant element of the role was sales, and I didn't care for it; cold calling businesses was like selling your soul to the devil, but what I did care about was helping people find work. It 100% was the saving grace from the life I had been living.

I didn't know what manifesting I was back then, but now looking back on it, I for sure manifested the next job I landed in recruitment! I'd just split up with my boyfriend of 4 years, and I was desperate to find a job that lit me the fuck up! I applied for a job working for a company in the utility sector. It was an internal recruitment job, and I got it! There were 7 of us who started at the same time, and the job was an absolute dream! I travelled the country, staying in Hilton hotels hosting recruitment days for Sales Representatives. All I had to do was turn up and do the interviews! I didn't even need to find the candidates, as this was all done for me. It was the perfect situation and job; it was exactly what I needed! I was good at something for the first time in a long time. I was succeeding in THE ideal job! Week after week, I produced the highest figures out of all seven recruiters, and the praise I got was incredible! It was one of the highlights of my career, and I'm forever thankful for the opportunity. It finally gave me a purpose and a lot of my 'why'. Little did I know this was the springboard to my creating my own recruitment business!

From the ages of 24 to 38 saw myself in toxic relationship after toxic relationship. It was like a conveyor belt of the shit situation after shit situation. I was so blindsided by any asshole that would show me the tiniest breadcrumbs of affection. I would be so desperate to have some form of connection with them that I would commit myself to a relationship that would ultimately end up with me being hurt or cheated on. I used to say regularly, "I'm an asshole magnet" little did I know then that I was utterly telling the universe to give me more of the same situation!

The guys I attracted were just more excellent versions of my dad. I was drawing all that I thought I was worth, and I just wanted to hold that version of me that thought she wasn't good enough and squeeze her tight and make her see that she was worth so much fucking more than she ever put up with. Don't get me wrong, some super lovely guys also crossed my path, but I would toss them aside; I was just so tunnel-visioned on the 'bad boy vibes.

I finally stopped using drugs towards the back end of 2021. I didn't enjoy doing them anymore and hadn't done them for a while. I was mainly using them to get close to guys I was dating, I honestly used to think it gave me some form of street cred, some form of sex appeal as guys would think it was cool that I would party with them, but no relationship can be built on this, that I've learnt the hard way.

The BIG turning point for changing my life around was therapy. I started treatment back in 2020. The first therapist I started my journey with didn't get me anywhere. We started several sessions without resolution, and I terminated the relationship after seven months. I stumbled across another therapist by fluke, which made a difference. I was finally making headway on many issues, and it all started to make sense. The root cause of my problems was a lack of self-worth, but even then, it took me a while to start using the tools I was given to start putting my life back together. My therapist told me, "I can keep taking your money, but I will keep telling you the same things"! I knew my time in therapy was done after this, and it was time to put my big girl pants on!

March 2022 was a pivotal moment for me. The month I finally said yes to me! Yes, to leave the last and final toxic relationship I would ever be in. Yes, to finally put me first! Yes, to start a new life! I had checked out of my last relationship a good six months before leaving it. I had developed a close bond with his kids which made it even harder to go, but I knew I was worth so much more than the mediocre attention I was getting and the way I was being treated. I packed up and started a new life, one of the hardest things I've ever done; it was a dark six months getting myself back to a place where I felt like myself again.

I've always felt a connection to spirituality; I could feel something calling me, something bigger than me. I felt a strong knowing that life had something to show me that I wasn't experiencing, and everything had led up until this point. I had a spiritual awakening! I spent weeks feeling numb and alone, but little did I know the bright and beautiful path was about to unfold.

I had dabbled in online courses, which helped me to embark on my journey into spirituality, but it wasn't until June 2022 that I came across a lady that changed my life, Shamina Taylor. A post of hers on Instagram spoke to me on so many levels; after exchanging messages, I joined her container of like-minded, super-successful women from all over the globe! Her online learning has given me an education I never knew I needed, changing my daily life. Investing in myself was THE best decision I ever made, and I've invested in several other mentors and healers who have helped me on my journey.

Summertime of 2022, I decided that my life needed to change even more. I drastically reduced drinking as it affected my mental health; even after two glasses of wine, I would feel so hungover the next day. I started taking control of my finances and working on my toxic habits and relationships with myself. I came off all the dating sites and committed to dating myself!

And let me tell you, this was such a revelation! To put myself first, to be selfish with my time and get to know myself has been life-changing! Christmas 2022, I treated myself to a £6000 holiday in Thailand. I travelled alone, which was one of my life's best experiences! I got to spend Christmas eve and Christmas day feeling and bathing elephants. If I had waited for a man to treat me to this experience, I might have never gotten the opportunity!

I set up my recruitment agency back in 2017, and it's something I am so fucking proud of. I named the business after my Grandad, and I love that I have something in his name. I had no idea what I was doing back then, but after being made redundant three times in a row, I had to do something to get myself out of this vicious cycle of constantly searching for work. I took that leap of faith, which so many others are scared to do, but I knew I would always regret this leap if I didn't make it.

For the first 12 weeks, I had nothing, no clients, and no money coming in. I was slowly giving up. I reached out to the client that had made me redundant with a 'Hey! If you need me, I've set up my own business, and boom! They gave me ten roles to work on! Relieved wasn't the word; they became my biggest client for around a year. Years two and three were all around learning how to grow a business, and after investing in some training on LinkedIn, I cracked the code for getting clients.

Years 4 and 5 were the years I made the most money I had ever made, even during a pandemic! This was down to my obsession with seeing my business succeed. I was not letting a pandemic take down a company I had worked so hard to build. I've never been so consistent and determined about anything in my life! But there's a dark side to running my own business; I was letting my business run me to the point that I had a couple of breakdowns because of the pressure I put on myself. I have no idea about the pressure to succeed, the pressure to prove something to somebody – who this somebody was, but I guess it was the validation I never got as a child, the praise I was always seeking.

Around September 2022, I could feel a calling for something that wasn't running my business as I had done for the last six years; I wanted to get creative! But I had spent six years creating a brand that I didn't want to let dwindle, so I put it out to the Universe to help me find another recruiter that wanted to work under my brand, and within a week, a South African recruiter contacted me. Three weeks later, we signed the paperwork! I've been in recruitment for 21 years, and the way I was working wasn't challenging me anymore.

I still work under the brand Hargreaves Recruitment, but now I get to do things that light my soul on fire! I get to work with businesses training them on how to do their recruitment, and I'm creating online programmes to teach others how to set up their recruitment agency and achieve the successes I have achieved! 2023 will also be the year I start to coach and mentor other recruiters in their journey and support them on all the challenges I have successfully overcome – it honestly makes me so excited that this gets to be my life!

I knew my life had to change and going to therapy and starting self-development was the beautiful and messy path that must lead me to create a life I am so proud of. It's enabled me to finally start loving and respecting myself after years of mistreating myself, to be my own best friend, to get out of my way, to stop people pleasing, emotional eating and being a victim, to set boundaries, to put me first, and, to trust in the Universe.

I practice self-development every day; it's an integral part of my life, which looks like this.

- Meditation (guided and silent);
- Breathwork (I usually do a 15-minute guided breathwork session on YouTube);
- Journaling (includes writing down all my thoughts, a list of everything I'm thankful for, my intentions for the day, I am celebrating all the good things happening in my life, and I write down all my deepest desires);
- Working with angel cards and a pendulum (I pick one

card each morning which I select with a pendulum. I am super connected to my pendulum, and it guides me each day with 'yes' and 'no' answers to questions I ask).

I can't tell you how many people tell me they don't have time to practise self-development that, are stuck in the same cycles as I used to be and are deeply unhappy in their lives.

We all can make a difference in our lives and to create something magical, but it takes commitment, leaving the old version of you behind that doesn't serve you anymore and putting your trust and faith in the universe.

These last 12 months have been the most significant commitment of my life, and I wouldn't change a single second.

It all starts by going within.

It all begins with putting yourself first.

It all starts with you.

About the Author

Leanne Makinson is the British-born founder and Director of Hargreaves Recruitment Ltd, which she created back in 2017. Leanne is 39 years old, and a proud dog mum to a beautiful two-year-old Cane Corso named Koba.

Leanne was a self-acclaimed wild child. She had substance abuse problems for most of her 20s and 30s. She had failed in most parts of her life and romantic relationships until finally admitting she needed help and started therapy in 2021. She then embarked on a journey of self-development, finally beginning to love herself, beating crippling anxiety and discovering her self-worth. She is now creating a new version of herself, one that puts herself first. She now dates herself and is training to help others heal the way she taught herself to heal.

Email: Leanne@hargreavesrecruitment.com
LinkedIn: www.linkedin.com/in/leannemakinson
Website: www.hargreavesrecruitment.com

Lisa Dias

The White Picket Fence

"Your life is perfect! You have everything! You are so lucky!" These are the words that constantly reverberated in my head, spoken by my closest friends repeatedly throughout my childhood.

For the most part, they were right. I had loving parents and extended family members, amazing friends who, even now, three decades later, are still like family to me. They became the soundtrack of my childhood years. I attended a small but friendly primary school in the Eastern suburbs of Brisbane, which was popular with students and teachers. I was selected as School Vice-Captain, Sports House Captain, Student Councillor and Music Captain. From outward appearances, everything looked perfect, and it was. Though you never truly know what is going on the other side of the white picket fence.

Like most kids in the 1990s, I spent most of my days playing outdoors. I would ride my bicycle with friends to our local parks, rope swinging and jumping into the Brisbane River without truly knowing what was beneath us. We drank water from hoses, ran naked through sprinklers, climbed trees, hung upside down from monkey bars, played endless games of hide and seek, tiggy or bull rush, swam in pools and stayed out everywhere and anywhere in our neighbourhood most afternoons until sunset, or until our parents finally decided it was time to call us inside. As I said, it was perfect and some of the greatest moments and most cherished memories I have held my entire life. Suddenly, adolescence hit and along with it came many challenges and changes.

Although popular in primary school, this soon changed once I started High school at an all-girls school. The friends I had made at primary school soon made friends with others who had very different values and ideas from what I did. Following a spate of bullying, I soon left the group and found myself bouncing around like a yo-yo from group to group, searching for the people who were most like me. My kindergarten friend also attended this high school, and I was eternally grateful when she welcomed me into her group with open arms. This reinforced our friendship and strong bond, which to this day, is still a highly valued and treasured friend to me.

Once I had established myself and was comfortable with myself in this new friendship group, I began settling into school life and the more social side of things. I attended many 'blue light discos' as they were known then, run by our local

PCYC club. I also attended many dances at the local boys-only schools and even began to date a few of these boys, some lasting longer than others. I also started attending many parties and gatherings with colleagues and friends that I had made from my part-time job at Hungry Jack's. I was active in my sports and continued to pursue my love of netball, which featured prominently in my primary school days through school and club. I also regularly attended swimming squad training most mornings and afternoons.

It was around 15, however, when my so-called 'perfect life' began to unravel. One afternoon I was walking home from school from my back-door neighbour's house. My mum had gone back to full-time work, and since my neighbour's daughter was also attending the same high school as me and we were friends, she offered to bring me home with her in the afternoons. I would walk from their house, through the back gate into my backyard, through my side gate and then enter the front door of our two-storey Tudor-style house. Easy! Well, so we thought.

On this particular afternoon, as I entered my backyard and approached my side gate, I noticed my 30-something-year-old next-door neighbour smiling at me. Being the polite and friendly person I am, I smiled and said 'Hi'. He then proceeded to come towards me to speak to me. Even though I had been his neighbour for 15 years, we had never spoken before this, other than a brief wave, smile or 'Thankyou' on the days that my netball accidentally flew over the fence and had to be retrieved from his yard. In a few moments, I was about to understand why.

'Hi, I'm Michael,' he said. I've lived beside you your whole life. 'Yes, I know,' I replied. 'I'm Lisa; nice to meet you'. Then he said something to me that still makes my skin crawl. 'You're a beautiful young girl Lisa. I've been watching you growing up. 'Ok, thank you', I said, wondering where he was going with this. 'I've been watching you from my balcony when you come outside.

When you were little, you used to swing upside down from your monkey bars, and I would see your breasts and underwear when your dress lifted.' By this stage, the colour had drained from my face, and I thought of making a swift move inside before I either vomited or passed out.

I think I was possibly frozen in shock because I didn't go anywhere, and unfortunately, he continued. 'I love to watch you when you go swimming in your tight togs and bikinis. I want to take you and make you mine.' Turning and moving towards the gate to go inside, I say, 'Thank you, but I have to go now'. Then he said a sentence that I have never forgotten. 'Do you wish your parents were dead?' Stopping abruptly in my tracks, I turn around and reply. 'No, I don't. Why would I? I really have to go.' Promptly, I walked through the gate and went straight inside the house, double-locking the doors behind me.

Oh my goodness, I have a stalker. Not only that but one who wants to kill my parents and take me and make me his! Safely inside, I immediately got on the phone and called my mum at work to tell her of my encounter with the neighbour. This is where I found out that he not only has schizophrenia and was currently off his medication but that he owned a gun and was well known to the local police and hospitals. With genuine concern that he could harm our family and make real of his threats, the next few minutes entailed the police being called and a 'flag' being put on our house so that any calls which came from us would be answered with great urgency. My back-door neighbour came over to be with me until mum and dad got home from work, and I was placed on 24-hour supervision. My school and other places were notified of our situation so that if he attempted to come to my school, netball club or friends' houses, the police would be called immediately.

The next few months saw our beloved house sold and our family packing up and moving to the bayside suburbs of Brisbane, known as the Redlands. Whilst I remained at the same school to complete my schooling, my daily trips to and from school now included catching both a bus and a train each way—a small price to pay for my and my family's safety.

Do you believe that you are meant for more? That you were put here on Earth at a specific time for a particular purpose? One day when I was 19 years old, I had my red Holden Nova in for a car service at a service centre just a couple of kilometres from home. I decided to walk down to pick it up when it was ready. I started walking to the service centre when I received the phone call. It was a beautiful sunny day, and I was excited to exercise.

About halfway to my destination, as I walked along Rickett's Road, a car on the opposite side suddenly slowed down, did a U-turn across the middle lane, and slowly started creeping up behind me. I saw what it had done and turned around to stare at it. It stopped. I turned around and continued walking. As I walked, it continued slowly following behind me. I stopped again and turned around. Again, it stopped. I turned around and again continued walking, this time getting out my mobile phone and car keys in preparation for anything which might be about to happen to me.

Suddenly out of nowhere, a white van pulled across in front of the car that was following me, and the driver began to read it a map. I waited for a few moments near this white van, watching the car to see what would happen next. Suddenly, the car roughly pulled out from behind the white van and sped off down the road. I wait for the car to be well out of sight before I continue my walk down the road to the service centre.

This day, I learnt to believe in Guardian Angels and Higher

Powers. I know that I would not be here today if that white van had not stopped when it did. Each day I thank God for his divine intervention in my life and take it as a sign that I am meant to be here for a higher purpose doing great things. I do not know who was in the white van that day, as I never got the opportunity to stop and thank the man for saving me from a likely kidnapping. So if you were the person in the white van that day and are reading this, from the bottom of my heart, I thank you. I often wonder whether the person in that car was my ex-neighbour Michael and what might have happened to me that day.

Like the lyrics from Ronan Keating's song, 'life is a rollercoaster, you just got to ride it', the next few years of my life were filled with some of the highest highs and several belly-dropping lows.

In 2005 I enrolled into university, and four years later successfully completed a Bachelor of Education. Soon afterwards, I entered the teaching profession as a relief teacher. I fell in love with my now husband, and together we have had two beautiful girls whom we love more than words on a page could ever express. Sadly, over the years, I lost all 4 of my beloved grandparents and our beautiful 14.5-year-old dog, a Maltese called Bundy, who had been my best friend and companion for literally half my life. I take comfort, though, knowing they are all still around us, surrounding our family with love, guidance, and blessings from above.

Following the years of being a stay-at-home mum and raising my kids, I returned to the workforce, deciding to change directions, and moved into aviation. Up until the pandemic of 2020, I enjoyed 6.5 wonderful years at one of the top airlines in Australia as a Guest Services Agent and Operations Planner. I met some of the most amazing people I am incredibly grateful to call my friends, enjoyed six family holidays to Fiji, amongst other places, and met the most significant number of celebrities you could list in your lifetime. Still, I promise not to brag about it here.

Following the pandemic, which brought the aviation industry to its knees and my beloved job was made redundant, I faced the challenge of 'do I return to teaching, wait for the aviation industry to re-start, or find something else?' Whilst being stuck at home for more than six months, I was introduced to the beautiful professions of network marketing and coaching.

I had already been introduced to and dabbled in them several years prior when one of my closest friends was a Tupperware consultant, and another asked me to join her in a health and wellness business. At the time, however, I believed I did not have the skills or abilities necessary to 'be a salesman' or make real money in these ventures. Like many people's opinions, I also believed them to be scams.

However, I soon learned that I could not have been more wrong. After closely following a high school friend of mine on social media, I saw that she was working from home, around her daughter and running a very successful online business. She had not only lost a significant amount of weight, but she was also coaching others on how to achieve the same results in health and business. I had to reach out to her to find out more. She introduced me to her Breakthrough coaching program, which included health and wellness, a money mindset, personal development, social media, online business strategies and marketing. I had never seen anything like it before, and after promptly investing some money, I commenced her 8-week breakthrough program.

The results I achieved were incredible. After just eight weeks, I had lost approximately 5 kilos through better eating and exercise habits, worked through some personal mindset blocks, developed a healthier relationship with money, and created a business plan to build and release my coaching program. I made many new like-minded friends who actively encouraged and supported each other to become the best versions of ourselves we can be.

Witnessing the results for myself, I was hooked. I knew I just had to learn more about this industry and find out how so many 'average' men and women were making six and 7-figure salaries and retiring their spouses.

Full disclaimer: the coaches and network marketers making these incomes worked hard for their results, and success is not easy nor guaranteed.

The next few months saw me join 'Rankmakers'- a training and support group for network marketers. Through high-quality training led by Ray and Jessica Higdon, I achieved more success in my network marketing company. This increased my confidence, and I knew I could do this! Soon afterwards, I joined their "Inner Circle" coaching program, where I was assigned a highly successful business coach and strategist named Elsa Morgan.

I am a massive believer that God places people and blessings into your life for a reason, and Elsa Morgan is one of them. This brilliant, beautiful, and talented woman locked arms with me. She showed me exactly how to build a personal brand, sell with authenticity and without having the stinky commission breath, attract incredible clients and customers, and build a business around my kids, husband, and lifestyle step-by-step. We would have frequent one-on-one business calls, and I also participated in numerous group coaching sessions. The results spoke for themselves! I recruited my first of several team members into my business, and the number of sales from customers who bought from me also increased.

To add to these successes, in 2022, I invested in an NTT (Neuro Transformation Therapy) program by Luke Hawkins. The program helps you to learn the art and science of creating lasting change in your life by mastering your inner and outer worlds. Over the course of 4 12-hour (or more) days, I worked with many coaches and trainers to complete the program and attain my certification as a Neuro Transformation Therapy practitioner and coach. This certification allows me to help people to break through their fears and limiting beliefs and create lasting change in their lives by utilising the power of the subconscious mind and changing how we communicate with ourselves and others.

Upon learning these skills, I started implementing changes in how I communicated with students, colleagues, and many other people I interacted with daily, and I noticed some fantastic results. I saw that I could control the challenging behaviours of some of the most demanding students within schools just by changing the way I spoke to them. Simple changes in how I communicated with students allowed me to positively influence their thoughts, feelings and behaviours, allowing me to have better control of the more potent behaviours in my classes and positively increase the amount of focused teaching time. By this stage, I was hooked and had to learn more.

Later in the year, I again invested in an NTT Mastery program from Luke Hawkins. This program delved further into mastering the skills to bring about personal breakthroughs and create lasting change in coaching clients. It also introduced me to Timeline Transformation Therapy, which allows me to help clients to release negative emotions, fears and limiting beliefs and create positive and lasting change in their lives. Following another set of 4 (12-hour) days and working with multiple coaches and trainers, I completed the program and gained my Master of Neuro Transformation Therapy practitioner and coaching certification. I could not be prouder of myself for what I have learnt and the skills I have gained from these fantastic training programs. I am also incredibly grateful to Luke Hawkins for his endless support, guidance, and encouragement.

This brings me to today. I continue building my network marketing business and supporting women to achieve their health and wellness goals. Next month, I will launch my signature coaching program, 'Recalibration', which helps women to remove their fears and limiting beliefs and instil the new beliefs and behaviours needed to reach their potential and ultimately live the life of their dreams!

I am so excited for the future and cannot wait to fulfil my vision of impacting 1 million women.

About the Author

Lisa Dias is a qualified teacher, certified Master of Neuro Transformation and Timeline Transformation Therapy Practitioner and Coach. She is wife to Kris and mother to her 2 children, Sophie and Katherine.

Lisa grew up an only child and she learnt that life wasn't all roses and white picket fences. During her teenage years, she overcame the challenges of being stalked and later, an attempted kidnapping.

Lisa's resilience and tenacity shone through to overcome her traumas and become the first member of her family to graduate from both High School and University.

Lisa is the Founder and CEO of Lisa Dias Coaching. Her signature program 'Recalibration' helps women to remove their fears and limiting beliefs, whilst instilling new beliefs and behaviours to help women to reach their potential and ultimately live the life of their dreams!

Lisa is determined and driven to impact 1 million women globally through her coaching business.

Facebook: www.facebook.com/profile.php?id=100089360937145

Lyndee Nicholson

'Women Who Could, Should'

When the term 'Network Marketing/MLM' was uttered in conversations over a decade ago, the entire concept was foreign to me. I remember receiving a flyer in our family's letterbox as a 19yr old. I was sceptical yet also curious. My father had some choice words to say about non-traditional business, and he quickly pointed out that it was probably some pyramid scheme or a scam. He discarded the flyer, but I must admit that I still have the flyer in one of my packing boxes at home.

Decades later, I met a person who knew the woman who had generated that flyer – the most senior female entrepreneur in Australia in the company that I now represent. How fortuitous is that? I believe that when the student is ready, the teacher will appear; for me, that was in 2004.

My initial interactions with an MLM representative was through a neighbour, as she could see my struggles with my various health issues (2004). I don't recall having the best introduction, not by any fault of my neighbour but of the 'over the top' representative who was very dramatic and 'salesy'. I was, however, drawn to her products but then proceeded to exit as quickly as possible as she was very pushy. My excitement waned after she drove to my house, got her son to deliver products to my door, and then sped off down the street. This left me disheartened, so I stepped back after being a loyal customer for over a year.

There was a pivotal point in my life where I knew I needed to get healthier outside, although I am now aware that inner work is more important. Shortly after losing weight, I was introduced to another kind and genuine consultant. She offered me the opportunity to become an active member (2006). I was shocked! At the time (2004), I was struggling financially and trying to cope with a six-month-old baby with breathing/apnoea episodes and young disabled twin boys. I wasn't aware I could work independently, let alone take advantage of company benefits. Emotionally I was going through a divorce, could not pay my rent and knew that the likelihood of all 3 of us living in my car became very real. Had I been asked if I was dissatisfied, my life may have taken a completely different turn. I was keen to engage in a new adventure and start a new life. Suddenly, I felt my world begin to open, a weight lifted off my shoulders, and I realised that there was hope for my future. To this day, I always make a conscious effort to build relationships and trust with my customers/team members due to the representative's caring nature.

I was very reluctant to write my story. I love hearing about everyone else's adventures but rarely discuss my life. Whilst I admit I'm a social butterfly, you'll typically find me reflective, curled up on the lounge looking out to my garden where the sunlight catches a few colourful flowers in my garden beds, with a cuppa in hand, reading one of my many personal development books. I'm unsure whether my story will be your cup of tea – we'll see!

I am the youngest of 4 girls, raised on the Northern Beaches of Sydney, NSW, Australia. I come from a down-to-earth, fun-loving family. Most of my family members were/are all well-educated - artists, salespeople, lawyers, farmers, doctors, veterinary surgeons, dentists and a politician (Minister for Transport PNG, who was Knighted by the Queen) ... and then there's me – the intrepid traveller, an ongoing student with a love of complementary health and eastern philosophies!

As a teen, I enjoyed fun times at the beach, the sand between my toes, had a sun-kissed tan and blonde hair, and loved swimming beyond the breakers in the ocean and connecting with many friends. We would giggle for hours and repeat the same activities the following weekends at various beaches along the peninsular. We engaged in many outdoor sports. Our healthy, active lifestyle was an expectation, not a choice. We didn't have exposure to digital communication or mobile phones. In fact, what always sticks with me is this: I always kept 20c in my pocket to contact my mother from the phone box (yes, they existed) – 2 rings, hang up, two rings, hang up – meant Mum would collect me at a specific location. I didn't have to ask for money the following weekend unless I spent it on lollies! If so, I'd have to trudge for 45 minutes up a very steep hill until I reached home. We hit the ground running without a care, experiencing life and all it had to offer.

Born into a middle-class family of 1 professional parent, the other a homemaker doing her best to navigate the challenges of having profoundly identical disabled twin daughters, life was sometimes often for me on weekdays. I learnt at an early age to entertain myself, work diligently at school, research projects at the local library for assignments, play with our dog and enjoy cooking. I always had a view of 'wanting more' but never vocalised it.

If you can imagine a large sketchpad, then this is where I scribbled drawings of what I wanted my house to resemble, my ideal car, family, pictures of travel destinations from National Geographic magazines, tailored clothes, classic cars, great friendships, surrounded by animals and an extensive vegetable/herb garden. My biggest goal then was to be a mother giving them all the love they needed, drawing on all my unique experiences. I loved my visual stories. I asked for six kids and got 3 – that was enough! As I matured and entered relationships, my drawings were seen as a waste of time, so I discarded them, ultimately shying away from any attempts (at what I now know was goal setting) for over 30 years. Until my introduction to network marketing, I had no idea how integral goal setting is.

Developing foreign language skills over the years proved to be essential for my nomadic, backpacking, intrepid lifestyle. My parents encouraged me to enjoy life, be happy, the importance of working hard, be an honest, strong communicator, respect others (and treat others as you want to be treated), and how give without wanting anything in return. This was evident after my father received an O.A.M (Order of Australia Medal) in the late '80s for Services to the Disabled at Government House, Sydney, NSW.

After leaving high school, I had no idea what I wanted to do except that I knew I had a passion for travelling and hoped that some day, I could incorporate that into my work. Exposure to other cultures emerged from a passionate educator at high school who immersed me in his visualisations and exciting global adventures. I chose to learn clerical skills to work in temporary jobs locally and globally to find what field I might gravitate to. What conspired were feelings of stress from driving 1.5 hours one way to jobs that I didn't enjoy, watching dissatisfied workers doing the same job day in/out and for myself and having an intense dislike for the 9-5 grind. The cost of petrol and parking far outweighed my hourly wage. Frustrations were plenty as I felt I was different, but I didn't know where who, how or what to start researching to get to 'there', whatever 'there' was! I went into the city for a week to learn how to 'sell encyclopedias' to gain different skills. It was definitely out of my comfort zone.

I spent over 30 years as an intrepid traveller, always gravitating back to Southeast Asia. I love their culture, bizarre foods, colourful festivals, huge crowds, families, the joy of life, noisy markets, temples, festivities, and their crazy drivers – **all** things **I avoid** in my own country! I love their sense of connection and community – something I try to apply in my business ventures.

During my 20s, I received an Advanced Diploma in Remedial/Sports Massage. I gained extra accreditation in other modalities to market myself differently to gain an edge in the marketplace. My first business was as a mobile therapist. When I became a mum of twins, I had to rethink my practice to allocate more quality time with the boys. My body was feeling the pinch of how physically demanding the work was. I ventured out as a Certified International Infant Massage Instructor (my 2nd venture, which I thoroughly enjoyed. Amongst all the mayhem around the twins' health, I authored two articles for 'Massage Australia Magazine' and numerous special needs articles for the Australian Multiple Birth Association (AMBA), which was a great honour – the latter of which are archived at Sydney National Library. When Maternity Wards/Prenatal Classes introduced infant massage classes into hospitals, retention drastically dropped, mainly when the Department of Health offered free classes. For some time, I travelled to outback NSW country areas, either lecturing or conducting classes in infant massage, but ultimately, it wasn't a viable option.

After my first marriage ended in 2007, I had $10 in the bank, outstanding rent and an unroadworthy car. Life was tough. To say it was tough was an understatement. I was a single mother of 3 children with complex medical issues. I would go for days only eating an apple to allow me to put food on the table for the children. I reverted to previous habits – listed all of my capabilities/hindrances, scribing until an idea would evolve.

… and then came business No. 3! An online gluten-free business. That worked a treat to the delight of my stomach and for my customers. My friend reminds me of the time that I put on my best clothes and make-up and had my 'red riding hood basket' with samples walking around the local shopping centre trying to drum up business. I sat in my car crying and shaking for nearly an hour, trying to get the courage to even step out and put a foot on the ground. Eventually, I began receiving regular orders; however, within six months, a customer sourced goods from my wholesale supplier. My business took a nosedive along with my ego. I took heed of what 'not to do'. My conclusion – always leave people 'wanting more'. There's an old saying: 'you talk ... then stop' ... my mouth didn't get that memo!

I relocated to Queensland in 2010 when in my first year, I survived one of the most horrific floods since 1979 and, for the second time, found myself on the precipice of being homeless once again. I stepped back for months, doubting whether I would ever achieve my goals. Not wanting to keep still, I needed to occupy my time. Between making party cakes/cake pops for families and hosting international students, I toggled two businesses – making creative birthday cakes and selling 'true blue Aussie gifts' to international groups/visitors. Business No. 4 arrived!

So what attracted me to Network Marketing? Initially, it was the flexible hours, working around my family's needs, no peak hour traffic to navigate, global opportunities, working with people I like, a scope to create any avenue that would suit my lifestyle and an honest way to remain open-hearted. Ultimately I learned how to build relationships with customers/team members.

You're probably thinking, but didn't you start your Network Marketing business back in 2006? Yes, that's correct, but I didn't have the support of my partners during that time, so my network marketing business was all very clandestine. It wasn't until I was single in 2016 and residing in Canberra (the capital of Australia) that I reignited my passion for wanting to help women like me, particularly those who are housebound with special needs children. The special needs arena can be very depressing, with varied horror stories that are undeniable. Yet, I want to impact future leaders and pull them out of the self-sabotage rabbit hole. I strategise my business annually, which is essential to find flaws and to help me amend trouble spots. It's a little like driving your car to a destination, but the satellite navigation takes you to a completely different area. You are faced with roadworks, so you change direction only to find that you were concerned for no reason. Your focus was on the goal, and you arrived, but from a path you hadn't even considered.

Is Network Marketing easy? It's what you want it to be. The fundamentals are easy to apply, but inconsistency is your enemy. Treat your business like a business, schedule your activities/appointments/times, ensure that your working area is conducive to production with minimal distractions, be authentically natural and get to it. Will there be hurdles? Absolutely but that's the joy of becoming the new you! Reinvention is critical to growth. Be accountable to a mentor/s, other entrepreneurs whom you can learn from, someone who knows how to take you into the scary zone for growth and embrace the change.

Two stories stand out for me. I met Karan whilst hosting

international students in Queensland. She struggled with severe migraines, lay in bed for hours, rarely saw sunlight and worked with her weight. She had little contact with friends, exacerbated by the fact that she didn't have a driver's license. Her husband was a shift worker, so they were like ships in the night.

"Lyndee visited my house discussing the benefits of her products, and I was amazed that after 24 hrs, I was out of bed with no migraine! It's comments like this that are so humbling. I am ever so grateful for the guidance and mentorship from the beautiful Lyndee. She was always there for help and assistance. If it wasn't for her, I don't know where I'd be today".

Another customer had been suffering joint pain for many years, exacerbated by the physical demands of being the primary carer for her elderly mother. It was such an ego boost to have someone pop in, collect any products and say, "make sure you keep that in stock; I didn't realise how problematic my pain was until I stopped ordering"! Even when I relocated interstate, we kept in contact through social media. She kept watching and would comment on my posts and me on hers. Today, she is one of my most loyal customers (after nearly a decade). My strategy is always to follow up, be honest and genuine, never judge, and be gracious and helpful.

Years later, I hit a roadblock that I wouldn't wish on anyone.

My daughter attempted suicide at 14 years of age. I can remember the 3 am wakeup as clear as day. Hearing those words, "mum, I've done something really stupid", still shakes me. In that wave of feeling alone, I questioned the events of the day, how, in that moment, how did I reach this point and trying to process what I had just heard her say and the words of the paramedic saying, "her intention was suicide and end her life". The impact of suicide is rough in itself, but more so with the knowledge that I also had two other family members who have taken their own life.

Through all my adversities, of which there have been many, I vowed to make a legacy for my children for them long after I've left the material world. Leading from the front with baggage from behind is difficult, so I work hard to build healthy relationships with clients and team members. Inner and outer have to work harmoniously, connect more regularly with my mentors, and continue reading, writing and disrupting my old schedules. 'Just do it' – are the words that always resonates in my head.

'My Mission'

To do what is right, not what is easy.

'Intelligent Design'

Master being kind to myself, learn to say no, set boundaries, work to a timetable, be adaptable and know that I have balance in my life in all areas – family, spirituality, work, friendships, health, exercise and continue being a student/learning.

'My Motto'

'Backwards is my New Forwards'

It makes perfect sense to me. It is imperative to break down 'doable' steps, so you don't become overwhelmed. Teach others this simple format. Duplication has a ripple effect….. therefore, it's my backwards plan!

'My Goal'

My role is to impact women who desire to get back on track after years of poor nutritional habits - whether self-inflicted or through failing lifestyles, particularly those with children with special needs. Educating women about healthy and well-informed choices can significantly impact their family's lives.

'Sparkle Unit It's Time to Shine

Keep persevering no matter what. Have a strong faith that '*you can do it*'. Be open to new ideas, e.g. 'grounding' or taking 'cold showers'. This, in particular, was extremely challenging, but now that I've settled into it, I've created a '*shower song*'! I look forward to feeling alive afterwards. Disrupt your '*normal*'. Keep your health in check. Exercise and enrich your mind/body through reading and meditation.

TOP TIPS:

1. Adaptability and diversity create new pathways – always be open to change

2. 4 x R's -set aside time nightly to *'reset, rethink, reflect and recoup.'*

3. Success leaves clues – connect with various leaders, lean into the unknown, grow through your mistakes

4. Create new habits – patterns expand your thinking and encourage exciting new neural pathways. Fire and rewire your brain through various mediums

5. Personal development – keep learning, writing, reading and listening. Magic happens when you least expect it, and who doesn't love magic?

About the Author

Lyndee is a mother of 3 children, including adult twin sons with profound disabilities. Her caring nature and genuine love for others is evident in her approach to work, life and leisure. In her spare time, she's an avid gardener with a wide variety of organic vegetables, herbs and fruit, and five chickens. Struggles with her children's health have not stopped her from becoming an entrepreneur. Lyndee's failure in multiple businesses has had a resounding effect on her, and as a result, she helps her customers improve and successfully navigate through challenges. She is a self-confessed foodie and animal lover. Travel is her stress-release and one of her many passions. Having survived many hurdles, she has chosen to focus on her health journey through many mediums - Pilates, reading, journaling, meditation, learning new languages and recently made the decision to return to college to learn complimentary medicine/nutrition.

Facebook: www.facebook.com/lyndee.nicholson
Instagram: www.instagram.com/lyndeenicholson

Maria Douglas

Discovering my purpose after adversity

I was born to immigrant Greek Cypriot parents in Melbourne, Australia. My parents were neighbours and childhood sweethearts. My dad came to Australia on a ship with one suitcase for a better life. He vowed to mum that he would work hard, make money and bring her to Australia and get married. True to his word, he worked in hospitality and saved enough money to put a deposit on a home and bring mum to Australia. She came on the ship, and they got married. My dad stayed in hospitality, worked as a chef at 5-star hotels and also started his own very successful restaurant in St. Kilda, a popular beachside suburb, amongst other successful ventures.

I grew up in a very happy household with an older brother. Dad was a very hard-working man and wanting the best for his family. He was very driven. Mum was mainly a homemaker and did some work. I always felt very safe, secure and loved.

Growing up, I would love pretending to be a teacher. I loved my blackboard & chalk. I would dress up in my mum's clothes and shoes, line up my cat and dolls on a couch and pretend they were the students and I was the teacher.

I was a conscientious student. I had skipped a year level at school and then also got a scholarship for being one of the top 50 students.

I took dressmaking classes, and I was learning the violin. I also went to Greek school.

My parents were strict. I mainly went out with my brother, my cousins and my best girlfriend, whose parents were also Greek Cypriot, and we had fun.

Fast forward, I got into Monash University, and I graduated in Information Technology.

Finishing in Information Technology, I then started work. A few years later, I was out. A good-looking, blonde-haired, blue-eyed guy came over to me and started talking. I said, "Do I know you?" He said, "No, but I'd sure like to get to know you! "

From that point, with this charming, handsome, attentive guy, I was mesmerised. Little did I know at the time, but this was going to be a crossroads moment in my life.

He swept me off my feet. He was the 'perfect' male! Almost too good to be true. He would continually tell me how he loved me; I was gorgeous, beautiful, smart. He was confident, extrovert, a big spender. I, on the other hand, was not that confident. I was more introvert and preferred to be in the background. Even though I had a good-paying career in IT and doing well, I played myself down and preferred to be in the shadows.

We started dating. I was receiving flowers, endless gifts, chocolates, dinners at great venues and his words of affirmation to me. He was obsessed with me and everything about me.

I was so swept up in all of this attention and receiving gifts I never stopped to question how little I really knew about him.

Within three months of seeing each other and me being caught up in a whirlwind, he proposed to me, telling me how much he loved me, I was the one and how gorgeous, amazing & perfect I was. Life was a fairy tale.

We got engaged, and he moved into my parent's home with me. He was keen to get married asap, so within the year, we were married.

When we got married, we moved into my home in Malvern. I had purchased this property when I started working before we met.

I wanted to do the "right" thing, so I decided to add him to the title of my property as co-owner.

Alongside all this, we had purchased two investment properties together in Malvern and a BMW.

I was very naïve and very trusting. Having been used to a father who was very hardworking, loved his wife and family and would do anything for us.

On the surface, everything looked like we were the happiest couple. When our life as a married couple started, I started to notice changes. He was drinking heavily when out. The compliments and all the attention I was getting became less and less. He started coming home later and later and was emotionally nasty.

Life went on, and I became pregnant. And with this, everything really started to change. He was out more at night with 'clients' for drinks for dinner, and I was no longer invited like I used to be. Then it became weekend conferences.

As my pregnancy went on, his interest in me got less and less, and now the nasty remarks started, such as, "How fat and ugly I looked ".

It was like this person was a total stranger with a double personality.

I couldn't tell my parents because I didn't want to worry them, and I couldn't tell my friends because I was embarrassed. So, I went to work and lived my life in fear and turmoil and pretended everything was ok.

I reached the point where I was suspicious. Where was he going? Why was he coming home 1 am, 2 am, and 3 am? I was too scared to confront him, and when I did muster the courage to do so, he would say he was at work and with work people, and why was I asking.

Around seven months pregnant, I would be driving around the streets of nearby popular nightspot suburbs at 1 am in the morning, looking to see if I could see his car anywhere, who was he with, what was he doing?

I knew something was wrong, but I had no concrete proof. I became like an obsessed detective hunting for clues. I was scared. I felt alone, helpless and trapped. I had to get to the bottom of it!

And then it came! The moment in time my life changed! A forever destiny moment. A moment in time, I had gone from being a passive, weak, stand-in-the-background female to a woman who stood up to fight for me and my unborn child.

It was a Saturday afternoon, and he was nowhere to be seen. I started driving around the streets of the neighbourhood, looking for a clue, where was he, who was he with? Then I spotted our BMW convertible, roof down on the main road next to a trendy café.

I parked my car and decided to go in! There he was! My worst nightmare staring right at me! He was sitting with a blond girl who was wearing my BMW cap. Their faces were a few centimetres apart, and they were staring at each other. I was absolutely gutted, devastated and angry. I marched over there, grabbed a glass of champagne sitting on the table, and I threw it over him. I started yelling! He denied everything saying they were just friends, to which the girl looked at me coldly and said to him, "tell her the truth! Why don't you tell her the truth!"

I stormed out of there, headed to our BMW, which was actually mine. I threw his and her bags that were in there into the street, got in the car, and drove off!

The next two months before the baby was born were difficult. Really difficult. He denied he was still seeing her. She kept ringing me and telling me he loved her and not me, I wanted him to leave, but he wouldn't. As I had decided to put him onto the title of my property, I was not able to get him out of the house.

The night I went into labour, I was sitting on the couch. Home alone. It was 1 am in the morning, and my waters broke.

Unstoppable!

At that moment, he got home. Everything happened so quickly. My contractions were coming in so quickly I had to get to the hospital. My beautiful baby daughter was born in a matter of one hour.

The next six months were hard. Still denying his affair and firing abusive comments at he, he wouldn't leave. I was back at work and had my baby to look after.

My whole world was crumbling around me. My parents and my brother were very supportive and helpful, albeit in shock, as were my friends.

One Sunday afternoon, he came home and was angry and became emotionally and physically abusive. I was scared for my life. I ran out the door to the neighbours to get help. The police came with their loudspeakers and blocked off the street. Over the loudspeakers, I could here, "Come Out, Come Out with your hands Up. "He had run out the back and jumped over the fence and ran off.

A protection court order followed, although this did not keep him away. I changed the locks; he broke the windows. He would come to work and let my tyres down.

At this point, I had something rise up in me. I was not going to let this take me down. I was going to stand up and fight for me and for my newborn daughter. I was going to come out of this situation bigger, better and stronger. I didn't know how, but I was determined to. I was no longer going to be a weak, stand in the shadows girl and quietly endure, playing down my capability and what I was worth.

Time to stand up and fight for me and my life and the life of my daughter.

I juggled work, a newborn baby, an aggressive ex-husband, mounting debt, and my instigating a divorce. I was drawing on an inner strength I didn't even know I had inside of me. Day by day, I was getting stronger, more confident, bolder, more resilient.

With the divorce settlement, so that I could keep my home, I took on a huge multiple 6 figure debt from the losses of our two investment properties sold, and I also wore the loss of the money he had been withdrawing by forging my signature. He walked away with no debts.

As painful as that was, it was a crossroads in my life. It brought out an inner strength, resilience, a feeling of being unstoppable and that I was not going down.

With my newborn baby daughter, I knew that I wanted to give her and myself the best life. I wanted her to go to the best schools and have the best things.

I got strong, even though around me was drama and upset. I was asking for something. I didn't know what, but just something to help me change my life.

At that time, there came another defining moment in my life when I had heard about Tony Robbins and how his events changed people's lives. I was at a friend's house with a group of females. We were all talking, and it was like the room went silent, and all I could hear was this woman talking about how life-changing Tony Robbins' events were.

As I was driving that week, I saw a billboard that Tony Robbins was coming to Sydney, Australia! That was my sign. I just had to go, no matter what! It wasn't easy to get there.

I made it after so many obstacles, and it was life-changing. Life really was never the same again for the better.

This event and the people opened up a whole new world to me. The personal development world. Positive people that wanted to achieve in life! Learning that we are capable of anything we want and that we can truly have and do anything we set our minds to!! I felt like I was renewed and reborn.

At the event, I met a friendly guy who became a trusted friend. He introduced me to some multivitamin and antioxidant products. Little did I know at the time he was going to be instrumental in the path my life was going to later take.

After I came back from Sydney, even with all the terrible drama still going on in the background with my ex-husband, my drowning in debt, raising my daughter, I was still so motivated. I was unstoppable.

I started to set my standards and goals high. I wanted to live in a beautiful home in the best areas, send my daughter to the best private school, give my daughter the best life, buy designer clothes, have investment properties and travel the world first class and stay in 5-star resorts. I also really wanted to make a positive impact on people's lives.

As a single mum, not receiving any financial support from my ex-husband, and also now heavily in debt, I decided that climbing the corporate ladder was the answer to achieving this lifestyle.

I became unstoppable and relentless in pursuing this goal. I was motivated. I just had to climb the corporate ladder and get those senior positions. I just had to.

I went on to have a very successful 25 year + career in Information Technology and in a male-dominated environment. I went from being a shy employee rising to the most senior ranks in my profession, reporting to the CEOs in blue chip companies.

I headed global teams of 300+ people. I had a multiple 6 figure income, bonuses, the beautiful big office overlooking the lake, a car spot and a personal assistant. I was also invited to 5-star events. I had great relationships with my colleagues, team members and other senior executives.

I went on to place my daughter in one of the most elite, expensive, prestigious private schools in Australia, and she was there for all her junior and senior school years. It was an awesome school, as was the school community.

Amongst our highlights with myself and my daughter at this time,

we travelled overseas on 5-star trips, yearly trips to the Gold Coast and Noosa, staying at 5-star hotels and beautiful local destinations like Portsea.

Other highlights with my daughter were travelling first class. From there on, we always flew business class. There was no going back. We stayed in beautiful 5-star hotels.

My daughter wanted to study acting at the New York Film Academy in Los Angeles, so I made this possible for her, and she worked hard. She lived in LA in a beautiful apartment which we furnished beautifully.

Alongside all of this, through my trusted friend that I met back at Tony Robbins several years earlier, I loved the products he introduced me to. My energy was great. I was healthy. I was getting compliments on my skin.

Then I discovered people in this company were creating the lifestyle I wanted – simply by sharing with others (part-time) – I started doing the same.

This resulted in me having an additional income. I would go to uplifting interstate conferences. The people were positive and supportive. I made some truly sincere and awesome friends, which I still have in my life today.

I also purchased investment properties and embarked on a huge property development. I made a lot of mistakes and caused myself a lot of financial stress and debt. I had overcommitted myself.

During this time, I had calls from creditors. I owed money everywhere. As a result, I ended up with a bad credit rating which was also going to cause me many issues for years to come. A lot of lessons learnt. I still love real estate investing, though, and I currently own 8 investment properties.

I had all my other goals outlined, and one by one, I would tick them off. It wasn't easy. I made a lot of mistakes. I learnt a lot and kept getting up, sometimes bruised and battered, but I kept moving.

During these years, my faith and journey with God became very strong. My deep faith kept me in the game and still does. I always put God first.

As time went on, I started to realize that success in Corporate came at a steep price: loads of stress, retrenchments, contracts finishing, long commutes and long hours. I longed for a life where I could be in control of my time – to make an income on what I thought I was worth, not what someone else decided.

The turning point came when I was asked to relocate interstate for my role. I didn't want to relocate. I also wanted to go and stay with my daughter in Los Angeles for three months, but I knew I wouldn't be given 3 months off.

It was decision time. That fork-in-the-road moment. Do I continue with my corporate career, walk away from my multiple 6 figure income, back myself and do my networking market business full time?

I decided! Time to say goodbye to the corporate world, head to the USA for three months and do my business full-time. I have never looked back!

The past four years has been extraordinary. I left Melbourne and moved to the Gold Coast. I have built a beautiful new home in Palm Beach, across the road from the beach. I can hear the waves at night.

I look back now, and I wouldn't change anything. Everything was happening for me, not to me.

I had faith that everything I went through was leading me to something bigger. I discovered I had a way to make a positive impact, a way to help people.

I've been able to earn income, travel the world, show people how to make money online through my network marketing business and also help people with their energy, health and anti-aging.

I have global customers and business partners. We travel together, do business together, have fun together.

I heard someone say this business is about turning strangers to friends, and friends to family. This is so true.

I am ready to support women who are looking for more in their life. Women who know they are meant for more. Better health, more community, more positivity, more fun, more money, more learning.

My vision is to impact 10,000 women globally through my online business and to also create a global charity for homeless children.

Are you wanting to start a business, or are you looking to make changes in your life?

Here are three tips that have greatly helped me with my journey:

1. Create a vision for what you want in your life. Focus on what you want in your life and where you want to go, not on where you are and your current results. Believe it's possible for you, even if you don't know the how.

2. Find mentors and a supportive community of people. People that will support you and your ideas, people that have achieved what you want. People that believe in you.

3. Do personal development. Our mindset is key to our success. Take responsibility for developing yourself and getting better every day. Be intentional with what you are learning and then implement.

If you're facing similar challenges as I was or if you would like to know more about how you can make a five and six-figure income online and create a life of your design and would honour me with reaching out to me, I would be happy to schedule a time with you.

About the Author

Maria Douglas is an Australian-born Mum to one beautiful daughter and lives on the Gold Coast, Queensland, Australia.

Maria moved on from an emotionally abusive marriage and financial loss to climbing the Corporate ladder. She left a successful multiple 6 figure Corporate career to pursue her own business.

Now living beachside, Maria is running her own business, helping women make money online so they can live a life of their design. She is also a passionate property investor with an international property portfolio.

Maria also loves to spend time out with her daughter, fine dining, out with friends, travelling and the beach.

Email: maria_douglas7@live.com
Facebook: www.facebook.com/maria.douglas.921
Instagram: @maria_douglas7

Marlo Fullerton

I remember it like it was yesterday. I was at my son's 6th-grade science fair walking around looking at the different booths and exhibits. My back was aching, I had sharp pains in my knees, my hips were burning, and I was even out of breath. I had to sit down and take a rest several times. This was the day that would change my life.

Hello, my name is Marlo Fullerton. I'm a wife to my amazing husband and high school sweetheart, the mother of two awesome kids. Our daughter is in her late 20s, and our son just turned 18 and is a senior in high school. How did that even happen…they grow up so fast. I am a software developer by day, and I have a work-from-home business that I am building around my family time. I was raised by my mom. My dad was never in the picture. I was very close to my grandparents, and Gpa was my father figure. We moved around a lot when I was young and finally settled in far up on the north coast of California during middle of high school, where I met my future husband in electronic class.

Now back on that day at the science fair, we had just gone

through big changes in our lives. We were both laid off and had to move from our beloved Montana to Southern Oregon to be closer to my grandparents in California as my grandma became ill. With one or both of us being out of work, we charged up all the credit cards and borrowed, and we did whatever we had to do to stay afloat. The bill collectors were calling, the stress was extremely high, and we ended up having to file for bankruptcy. It made me sick because we wanted to get back to Montana and buy a house. This was going to throw a big wrench in that dream.

During this time, my weight had crept up even higher, and I was at the heaviest I had ever been, and I was miserable. Sleeping at night was difficult because there was no comfortable position, and my hands were falling asleep. I was at the point that I could only wear stretchy leggings, and I couldn't even walk around my son's science fair or the grocery store, let alone do all the fun things we loved to do like go hiking, camping, playing volleyball and just running around playing with my kids. I felt like a failure as a parent and was afraid I would not be around to watch them grow up and have amazing lives if I didn't get my health under control.

It was at that moment, sitting outside the school resting my aching back, that I made a decision. I was not going to live like this anymore because I was not living. I was existing. I took out my cell phone and recorded a quick video of myself. It was dark, and you could barely see my face, but I told myself, "Remember this. Remember how you feel right now!"

That was it. It was like a switch had been flipped in my head. I was determined to get healthy, lose the weight, and live life to the fullest. When we got home, I immediately started searching for a healthy way to lose weight. I had been overweight most of my adult life and had tried nearly every diet plan and fad thing out there. Sure, I would usually lose some weight and sometimes a good 20 to 30 pounds, but I never stuck to it long-term, and the weight would always creep back up and then some. This time I wanted something I could stick to, and would be a lifestyle change.

After hours of searching on the Internet, I decided to change to a low-carb keto lifestyle. The three main reasons I chose keto are because I had done it before in the past and had success, it has the best variety and choices for what I like to eat, and there are a lot of health benefits besides just losing weight.

I started on my "Get Healthy Journey" the next day. I didn't know everything about doing keto, but I wasn't going to let that stop me or slow me down. I looked up the basics and learned as I went. I knew that having some accountability would really help me stick to it, so I decided to do a video every day about my journey. I talked about how I was feeling, how it was going, what I was learning, and soon I was sharing tips, recipes and reviewing keto products.

As the scale started moving downward, my clothes were getting looser, my back and hips were not hurting as much, and I could walk for longer periods at a time, but the most exciting thing was my blood test results. When I started, I was in the prediabetic range. After three months of doing keto and losing 28 pounds, my numbers were all in the normal range. It felt amazing to know I had made such a huge improvement in my health.

While I was continuing my health journey, I was also working on our financial goals. Our dream was to get back to Montana and buy a home on land with chickens and a garden and enjoy life. To do this, we had many obstacles. First, I was working part-time, and my husband was working off and on, so we needed to increase our income. Second, we needed to rebuild our credit after our bankruptcy.

I came up with a plan of attack. First, I created a budget and documented all expenses. You would be surprised how much you actually spend on all the little things. We applied for credit cards to establish good credit. Use them, but don't charge them all the way up, and always pay more than the minimum payments. And put something to savings every month, even if it is just a $1.

About the time I started my health journey, my grandma's health started to decline. She was recently diagnosed with heart failure, but they didn't have a good, estimated timeframe.

Could be over a year, may be a few months. I was trying not to think about that part. I was very close with my grandparents. My mom was a single parent, and my grandparents helped raise me. Gpa taught me to fish, and I learned so many things from them that have made me who I am today.

My grandma had taken a bad turn and had to go into the hospital and then into a rehab facility. My mom went down to help Gpa since he used a walker and couldn't get around very well. I took a turn to go down and help when my mom needed to go back to take care of things at her home. It was a 6 hour drive from our home in Grants Pass, Oregon, to Galt, just below Sacramento, CA. I felt pretty pathetic because we really didn't have the money for me to go down there. Gpa gave me the money to go down. I was glad to see her. She looked good and was in good spirits, and I was so glad to see she still had her sense of humor when she said, "I'm gonna hip hop out of this place!"

Gma was using a walker because she was short of breath and a bit weak, but she could get around. She had physical therapy sessions, and soon, she was able to go home. We were so excited. They got an in-home care worker to help both of them but specifically for my Gma. Anna was a godsend. She took such good care of them. I am thankful to her every day.

Sadly, my grandma only lasted a couple of months. Thankfully, I was able to talk to her on the phone many times.

I wanted to be there before she passed, but we were not sure when. Hospice was there, but I didn't really have the money for the trip and certainly not to make several trips. So, I waited, and we finally got a call to "come now," and I rushed down there in the middle of the night, but I was too late. She was unconscious when I got there. I didn't get to say goodbye while she was awake. I was devastated. How could I do that.? How could I not have the money to go whenever I needed to? I will never forget that I had let us be in this position.

She did not wake up again those last couple days. I sat by her side, hoping she would know I was there. At one point, when it was close to the end, I was hugging her, and I said, "I love you," and she turn to me and said, "I love you". She hadn't spoken or done anything like. I think she knew I was there, and she gave me that last goodbye. She passed the next morning.

This was a huge turning point for me. I was devastated I didn't have the money to be with my grandma before she passed. I vowed to never forget this and to do whatever I had to do to get our finances in order, to create a life of wealth where we don't have to choose between paying a bill or going to be with a dying loved one or friend. No more living paycheck to paycheck. I wasn't sure what I was going to do, but I knew I wanted to find ways to build multiple streams of income.

During all this, I was somehow able to stick to my healthy

eating and continuing to lose weight slowly but steadily. A big part of this was to do it not only for myself but for Gma. She had always wanted me to get healthy and lose the weight, so I was really trying to do it this time. I wanted her to see that I did it. I know she is watching over me and inspiring me.

About this time, I had a friend start talking about a health product that was helping her. I wasn't really interested at first, but she looked amazing, and she said it was helping her not only lose weight but gave her lots of energy, and she looked younger. Since I hit 50, I've been all about looking and feeling younger, and I could use more energy, so I decided to give it a try.

I started using the product, and to my surprise, it started to work. I had more energy to get things done, and my weight loss continued to break through a big plateau. I also noticed that I was losing more inches than weight. I started getting compliments on my skin and how fast my hair was growing. I felt amazing.

Then, I discovered that my friend and other people were making money from it, working their business from their phone around their families and life. What? This is awesome and exactly what I was looking for. I could work the business around my regular job to build an extra stream of income.

I got signed up and started building my business online

alongside my weight loss journey. I lost a total of 86 pounds and started playing volleyball again and hiking, and enjoying life. I continued to work on our financial goals as I was building my business.

Another important factor in my journey was working on my mindset and self-improvement. Most everything in our life is determined by our mindset. I started following mentors and taking courses to level up my mindset around money and wealth, and everything in my life. I started going to events and hired coaches.

For one event I got to fly to Florida. I will never forget the moment I got in my seat, and my seatbelt latched shut. OMG! The last time I had flown was before I started my health journey. I was almost in tears because the seatbelt did not fit. I needed an extender, but I was too ashamed to ask for one. I just tucked the seatbelt under my belly and pretended it was latched. I was horrified. But not this time. Now, it fits! It really fits. This time it was tears of joy.

Fast forward to today, and I have been able to build my business, earn and income online, and attract customers that love the products. And the best thing is being a part of our amazing community of like-minded women.

With the help of my business, savings, and a little luck, we were able to rebuild our credit and purchase a home with over an acre of land in Montana. It is our dream and a work in progress, and we are enjoying the ride. We have chickens, a beehive, and when in season, we're growing a garden full of vegetables and lots of flowers. This year we will be expanding the garden, and we now have a large green house. We were able to add a large shop/garage last summer and have many more projects to work on next year and the years to come. On top of our dream home, we also purchased our dream vehicle—a Jeep Gladiator Rubicon. I have to pinch myself every time I get in it and have the biggest smile on my face driving my Gladiator getting all those Jeep Waves. I am happy and grateful for this every day.

Now we are expanding our goals and our vision to purchasing more property, moving our family here, and setting up a foundation to help those in need. I am sharing these things not to brag but to inspire you to know what is possible and let you know that if I can do it, you can too.

I am still on my health journey, of course, because it is a lifelong journey. There have been a few bumps in the road, but the whole family is working on it every day.

Whether your goals are health-related or financial-related, the first step to getting anything you want is to decide to do it. You don't have to know how just know you are going to do it.

I did not know how I was going to lose the weight and get

healthy. I had "tried" many time before. This time, I made a decision I was going to do it. The how presented itself.

I didn't know how we were going to buy our home in Montana. In fact, although we were working on rebuilding our credit and budget, I still felt like we couldn't do it. I had that "we have bad credit" mindset. And telling myself, "we can't get financing", along with all the things we tell ourselves. Then the pandemic hit, and it lit a fire under my butt. We must get to Montana. I decided we are doing it. I started doing all the things. I called to get prequalified, I jumped through all the hoops, and there were many. We had doors slammed here and there, and I rerouted, and another door opened. Somehow the perfect house appeared in our price range where there had been none for weeks, and somehow, it was for sale by owner, and we were the first to get an offer in at a time when houses had multiple offers over asking price. We bought it long distance, only seeing pictures and a live video walk-through by our realtor. There were so many hoops to go through to get it all finalized and so many things that made us think…that was a miracle. Someone is watching over us. So many things had to line up, and we made it happen.

Once you decide, your mind sees things differently. How can I do this vs. I can't do this, or it will never work.

If you are working on your financial goals, figure out why you are doing it. What is the end big goal and dream. Make sure it is really an emotional thing that you can use to drive you. Decide you are going to do it. Then make an action plan. Get that budget tight, log all your expenses, build your saving, invest in yourself, build additional income streams to make it go faster. Be sure and work on it every day. Being consistent is so important.

If you are working on health goals, the steps are similar. Decide you are going to do it. Make an action plan and work on it every day. For losing weight, it is very helpful to log what you eat and things you do each day. This helps you find things that trigger you or stall your progress, then you can tweak. Be sure you are getting the proper nutrients and vitamins. Find supplements that work for you to assist in your goals and/or overall health.

In either case, remember that this is not a sprint, it is a marathon. It would be best if you were in it for the long haul. You didn't get unhealthy overnight, so you're not going to lose all that weight overnight, either. Same with your finances. Giving up doesn't get you there faster. You don't get there at all.

I want to show people through my online business how to get healthy, not only physically but financially.

My biggest desire is to help others see and believe that they can succeed and go after their dreams no matter what their present circumstances. My journey inspires you to get into action and go after your dreams.

I wish you all the success in your journey.

About the Author

Marlo Fullerton is a 54-year-old wife and mom of two children, four cats, three dogs, and 11 chickens. She enjoys doing DIY projects around her Montana property, gardening, and tending the chickens. Some of her hobbies are hunting, fishing, and driving her Jeep on the backroads.

She has been on a "Get Healthy Journey" for the past five years, where she lost 86 pounds and reversed her pre-diabetes.

She started her MarloGetsFit Facebook page to share her journey along with healthy tips and inspiration, and the community has grown to over 11,000 followers.

Her passion now is to help and inspire others to get healthy not only physically but financially as well.

Email: marlo@marlogetsfit.com
Facebook: www.facebook.com/MarloGetsFit
TikTok: www.tiktok.com/@marlofullerton

Melissa Sutherland

From broken…. to creating the life of my dreams

I walked into the room at an upscale country club, feeling self-conscious. It was my first quarterly event since I had given back my company car. My required uniform showed that I had lost my rank, and I felt deep shame and was dancing with depression. I felt that everyone was judging me. But I also felt determined to get back to my former glory and find my way. I made my way to the front row and sat down.

Quarterlies were a big deal in our company. There was no social media then, so it was how big rank advancements and car earners were recognized and given the chance to share their story. This event had visiting leaders from around the United States because they had local reps that had earned cars and become directors. There was so much recognition, and it should have been an opportunity to celebrate with women I cared for deeply. However, the event became a turning point in my life and one I sometimes feel emotional reverberations from today.

As my director, we'll call her Ellen, went through the recognition and various women began to speak, I remembered why I loved this. Why I was so proud to be a part of this organization. It was beyond money, although I wanted that too and needed it desperately because I was nearly bankrupt. How could I not be a part of something that was changing women's lives right before my eyes? My spirits were beginning to lift. Towards the end of the meeting, Ellen asked everyone who wanted to be a director to stand up.

I did not stand.

Not because I didn't want to be a director, I did with all my heart. You see, I did not believe I *could be.* My belief in my abilities was shattered. I was broke. My husband, Matt, was ready to leave me because of what he felt was my financial irresponsibility. I had lost most of my team. My precious car that I was so proud of was repossessed by the company because my business wasn't qualifying for it, and I couldn't afford the lease payment. I was 21 and felt broken and alone. I was not, in that moment, a director in my heart.

"Stand up, Melissa," Ellen demanded from the podium. I stood because I didn't know what else to do. Say no? That was unthinkable. I held Ellen up on a pedestal of success and wisdom and did whatever she told me, even if it felt wrong.

"Melissa, I want you to say I am a director!" Ellen said.

"I am a director," I said.

"NO! With feeling," She demanded.

"I am a director," I said more quietly.

"Try again," Ellen said.

"I am a director," I whispered.

Again and again, this happened until I was nearly in tears and feeling so embarrassed. When she got frustrated with me and said, "Ugh, never mind, just sit down." I felt such relief and humiliation at the same time. I felt like I was drowning from the pressure in my chest. I wanted to crawl into a hole and just die. I sat completely still the rest of the meeting, feeling the eyes of about 100 women burning into the back of my head. WHY did I sit in the front row? Why did I not walk out when she started demanding I say that? Why couldn't I just shout it out and end it?

As the meeting came to an end, I went to hug a friend goodbye before I made my escape, and her director pulled me aside. She looked at me with such compassion and said, "I don't know what your relationship is with Ellen, but she does not have your best interests at heart." And she hugged me. In that moment, I knew this was my last meeting, and I would not be returning.

In my time with that company, I saw it all. I was blessed to sit in the homes of multi-six-figure earners and millionaires. I saw the diamonds and the trips that could be earned. I saw all the glamour and the fun. I learned valuable sales skills and the benefits of personal development. But I also saw the behaviors that give network marketing a bad name. I experienced what I now know was emotional abuse and manipulation. I saw Ellen call people and pressure them to order inventory even if they didn't need it. I was made to feel less than on so many occasions, and because I was young and naïve, I accepted it.

I saw the possibility of success and walked away, deciding that was great for them, but it wasn't meant for me. Because I was not willing to do the things Ellen did to be successful.

As time passed, we had children and lived the beautifully rich life of middle-class working parents. I always found ways to monetize my hobbies because that was the only way I could afford them. I never made a fortune, but I made enough to cover what I wanted to do. We weren't poor, but we had just enough money, and that was it. That paycheck-to-paycheck lifestyle was not what I wanted for my life. I wanted more but couldn't see it happening. Life just was what it was, and with my husband and kids, I was happy, if not fully content.

After my dad passed from a heart attack at just 49 years old, I knew it was time to get healthy. I was overweight from having my son five years prior. I lost a forty pounds, and the universe rewarded me with a surprise pregnancy. She has been the biggest blessing, but the pregnancy weight gain was a struggle, and losing it was much harder in my thirties than it was in my twenties. A friend shared her product with me, and I signed up as a health coach "for the discount." I couldn't really afford the product, but I had a sales background and realized if I sold three packs a month, I would cover my cost. I could probably do that. So, I went to work trying. Network marketing was back in my life. And I quickly started to want more from it.

The first thing Matt said was, "this better not be one of those things again." And that hurt, a lot. Did he have no faith in me? I realize now he was justified to feel the way he did because it took me years to recover from the financial and emotional ruin of the first adventure. He had suffered the consequences of that experience alongside me. He and I are wired differently. I am the risk taker; he is the conservative one. We balance each other well and still love each other deeply after two kids and twenty plus years of marriage. But his words still left me feeling a little shattered inside.

I built a customer base and a small team. But I rarely earned more than a few hundred dollars in a month, and usually, it was less. I sent all the spammy messages. I posted obnoxiously on social media. I did free fitness groups. I would lay in bed at night asking God, "Why am I not successful? Why do these women who don't try as hard, study the products, know all the details of everything succeed when I don't? What do they have that I don't have?" I didn't understand that it was not knowledge of their product that made them successful but that they had the belief that I didn't. I had no faith in myself. Without faith and belief, success is difficult to find and impossible to maintain. I let comparison become a trap that I couldn't pull myself out of, and I felt myself becoming burned out trying to figure things out.

A lot of good came from that experience. I had leadership that was kind and not manipulative. And while not everything we were taught is what I would teach today, I never felt pressured to do anything that made me feel bad about myself. I never once felt humiliated, manipulated, or embarrassed. I fell in love with fitness and became a certified group fitness instructor and nutrition specialist. So, while I never felt truly successful in that company, I do feel like God placed me there for a purpose and a season. And that is where the shift began.

Five years ago, I found my current company through a Facebook party. I knew the rep from my previous company and thought the clothes were super cute. As a fitness instructor, I was constantly buying new things. Now being aware of network marketing "discount reps", I signed myself up, planning to cancel after I shopped. I did no research aside from reading the policies to make sure I could cancel whenever I wanted. I just went for it. But I was still living that paycheck-to-paycheck life. I had put it all on my credit card and knew I had no business adding to our debt. I told myself I would have just one party to make my money back. Drawing on my experience from my first company, I partied my heart out. I had so much fun! And I did make that money back. That on a whim purchase ended up being one of the best decisions of my life.

After doing well with my first party, I decided that I could maybe give it one more shot. And again, my husband said "this better not be one of those things." I was determined to show him the money. I was determined to show him that I had learned from my past. I was determined that this time was going to be different. I was not going to allow it to consume me, and I was not going to compare. I was just going to focus on selling cute clothes and being an affiliate. I sought out a coach because I wanted to learn how to sell better online without being spammy. And this is where everything began to change for me. Up until that point, it had never occurred to me to look outside my company for guidance. Why would I need a coach when my upline had all the training, and my company held events?

I had zero dollars to invest in one-on-one coaching, but I found a program that I said it could help me for twenty dollars a month and went for it. And I kept going. It was slow at first. I still had to learn that I was meant to have success. I had to learn to believe it was possible for me. I had to teach myself to dream again. Belief is a funny thing. Without it, nothing worked, no matter how hard I tried. But as I began to slowly build that belief, energy around my efforts seemed to shift and change. I was consistently selling, and even though I told myself I didn't want a team, I found myself with a small but growing organization. People are attracted to belief. As adults, so many of us have lost our ability to dream and believe, so when we find someone who has vision and positive energy, we are attracted to them. I was leveling up in my energy and building a community around me.

The day I earned director in our company, I was so excited! But that fear of losing it all came creeping back in. If I'm not successful, I can never again feel that humiliation of walking into the room, having lost it all. I wanted success, but I deeply feared repeating the experience of losing it.

About a year into my business, we decided to take a beach weekend, and being able to pay for that hotel out of my "business money" felt like a turning point in my belief and in my husband's belief in me. I earned that money, I paid for that hotel, and I made damn sure he knew it. And if I did it once, I could do it again. And I did. The consistency in action every day in my business led to more trips, more income, and eventually, my husband looking at me and saying, "I'm proud of you" while we were walking the beach in Hawaii. The day he posted about my business on his Instagram, I knew he finally believed fully in me. Together we have begun to dream bigger dreams and live a bolder life. We have seen that we are truly meant for more and take action together to make that happen.

Slowly and steadily, my business and my dreams have continued to grow. I have been invited to speak on team trainings and to lead company trainings. Never in my wildest dreams when I started did I imagine being called on stage as a six figure earner or making it to the top 2% of the company ranks. Rewriting the story of what was possible for me took time and consistent work, but really and truly, if I can do it, so can you.

The personal business success is exciting, but nothing lights me up more than seeing another woman succeed. As my team began growing and I had the opportunity to begin to mentor these amazing women, I found a higher calling in my life. I realized that I have more to give. It took me a long time to vocalize my desires, but as I whispered them to a few trusted women, I got resounding yesses from all of them. Again, I let that old fear of humiliation hold me back. One thing I have learned is that just when we think we have something beat, the universe shows it to us in a different way. Our programming, our beliefs try to sneak back in and keep us safe. If I never took the steps towards my dreams, I could never be defeated and humiliated again. So I let the calling to become a mindset coach sit and marinate for two more years before I took action.

Can we pause here and agree that 2020-2022 were a huge reset for most of us? Between lockdowns, changing work and family dynamics, constantly shifting economics, it was a lot to process, and I began to feel a little bit like I lost my way. I still loved my business and my life, but I felt stuck emotionally. I started studying spirituality and digging deeper into mindset work. And I realized that by suppressing the calling in my heart, I wasn't allowing God to work through me. I was stuck because I was no longer growing and believing in my ability to help other women grow.

My mindset coaching business is just beginning, and I have no idea where it will take me. I do believe that God has placed me here for a reason and that I needed to experience those seasons in order to help other women. My first two businesses weren't failures, they were lessons in the school of life. And shifting that belief takes them from the place of shame and humiliation to a place of elevation and learning. I'm now grateful for Ellen. While I wore the wounds of my time with her for many years, they are now scars. And you can teach others much better from a scar than you can a wound.

I am truly excited to step into the coaching space. The clients I am working with are women just like me. Smart, driven, and with families, they want more time with. And like me, they have the scars and wounds from the past that make stepping out into the unknown a little terrifying. As we identify what they really want from their lives and we begin to act, I have realized that we do for others in ways we won't do for ourselves. We encourage them to dream big and make their mark on the world while we hold back and let fear hold us hostage. We take setbacks as signs we shouldn't continue rather than opportunities for growth. We believe in them more than we believe in ourselves.

Building belief takes effort, but it is possible! Start with keeping the small commitments you make to yourself. If you commit to drinking a certain amount of water each day, drink the water and honor your word. The more promises you keep, the more you will trust yourself. Self-trust is the foundation of belief.

Another way to build belief is to celebrate your wins- even the small ones. Take a moment to do a happy dance when you achieve that small goal. When we allow ourselves to feel that pride and happiness, we are encouraged to keep going towards our bigger goals, and our belief in our abilities grows every time this happens.

Tap into a mentor or coach who can help you find any negative self-talk and help you shine a light on your strengths. Having a trusted person to hash out your goals, make a plan, and help you find ways around your obstacles is priceless! A coach will help you shortcut your journey, not be eliminating the work, but by helping you overcome the beliefs that will hold you back and slow you down.

Belief is truly what makes us unstoppable. Because if you truly and deeply believe in your purpose, you don't let setbacks stop you. The economy might change, the market might shift, there might be naysayers and people who don't support you. But if you truly and deeply believe in what you are doing and have a bigger vision for the future, nothing and no one will stop you for long.

Unstoppable belief leads to

Unstoppable vision which makes

Unstoppable action possible.

I believe in you and your ability to BE UNSTOPPABLE.

About the Author

Melissa Sutherland is a network marketing leader as well as CEO and founder of "Uplift and Impact Coaching," a life coaching and personal development business to help women get clarity on their goals, identify roadblocks, and make a plan to achieve those goals. Melissa has helped hundreds of women build marketing businesses and is now offering her skills to others through her coaching program. She has been recognized as a Rising Star in business, asked to train for her network marketing company, and spoken at industry events.

Melissa and her husband, Matt, have been married for 22 years and have two children, ages 12 and 18. They live in Florida with their dog and Melissa's 80lb tortoise, Shelly. Melissa is also an avid reader and loves paranormal fiction and personal development books.

Email: melissa@tummytuckleggings.com
Facebook: www.facebook.com/melissaasutherland
Instagram: www.instagram.com/melissaannsutherland

Rachael Hall

I grew up in a very Aussie, hard-working family in a little country town in NSW. Looking back now, we didn't have a lot of money, but my mother and father made sure we never missed out on much.

My mother always worked a very stable government job, your normal 9am – 5pm. I have always said my mother has the brains of the family. She knows everything there is to know about Math, English and loves reading. My father didn't work your "normal" 9am-5pm Gig, my father worked darn hard. Tuesday night was Paper night, he would start at 3pm Tuesday and sort the newspaper runs for all of the towns in the area. He would then come home around 3pm Wednesday afternoon. Monday, Thursday and Friday he worked at a local school as the grounds keeper. Come Saturday and Sunday, he would be refereeing soccer or be mowing lawns for extra cash.

My brother, now a Doctor, is three years older than me. My sister, now a Managing Director 1 year older than myself. Growing up, I would often joke that my brother and sister had Mums brains and didn't leave any for me. While they both breezed through school with top grades, I struggled. In year 6, I was reading and writing far below where I was meant to be. I was sent off to a school for four weeks in the big City, no family, no friends, just a phone call home every day and snail mail. I wouldn't say I liked it. I cried every night, however, I look back now and know it was all for my future. It was just a little chapter in my life. From going to the School in the City, I truly know now it was conditioning me to be better and strive for greater things.

Throughout my life everything I have wanted, I always felt as though I had to work harder than the person beside me. I always seemed to need help with new things.

Through high school, I landed my first job at a local eagle boys pizza shop. I worked darn hard for every dollar I made, however, I wouldn't say I liked it. I didn't like the little bit of money for the hard work, I didn't like having to report into someone every shift, and I wouldn't say I liked having to ask for time off when I knew the answer would be "No, we need you that weekend", so, at a young age of 14, I knew my future working years were not going to look like this. I watched on as my mother and father worked hard in jobs they didn't always enjoy, with long hours and hard work. I just knew in my heart I wanted a different path for my future.

At the age of 15, I was so blessed to be taken to Sydney and complete my first (of many) personal development courses.

This one, in particular, was a Bob Proctor seminar, 'You Were Born Rich'. For many years after, I would often find myself in Sydney with very similar courses. For myself, it put the spark in life. It made myself have a very clear vision and what I really wanted out of life. Not just work and money, but it has also helped me in my marriage, being a mother and my christian life.

After years of struggling at school with learning, direction and friendships. At the end of year 9, I told my mother and father school just wasn't for me. I wanted to work, and I knew my future. My mother then tried everything she could to keep me at school, she loved school, and my siblings were A+ students. Luckily my dad said, "Get a job and work and you can leave". My schooling years were over.

Fast forward, I married my best friend in 2011, and in 2013 we welcomed our first baby girl into this world. In 2015 my husband had a very stable job in the family business, running trucks, landscaping and much more. My husband's parents went through a breakup, resulting in the family business not being what it once was. I remember this chapter of our lives very well. We had a brand new car and a new family home, and life was great. I was a stay-at-home Mum, my husband made good money and supported us all. Life was as good and easy as it comes. With the break up came our own heartache; while we supported and loved both of my husband's Mum and Dad, the business where our wages came from wasn't coming like they once were. As a result, we had to sell our brand-new car, move into the business house and rent our home out. I still remember the feeling. I remember telling my husband it will get better, however, it didn't. I went to a café job while our daughter was looked after by an Aunty, my husband stayed working with his father however, it wasn't in town, it was in Newcastle, around 1.5hrs drive away. He would stay there all week, come home after 9pm Friday nights and work at the business on Saturday. We would see him one day per week. By this time, we also had baby girl number 2. It was at that point I said I have had enough. My husband had said he has also had enough. Our two girls hardly saw their father. I went searching, and when I say searching, I looked everywhere, I prayed and asked for help and asked for a sign, and an opportunity in Mudgee, NSW, had come up for us both.

We moved away from our families, work and the only life we both had ever known. Remember, we had no money to our name, no reliable car and two young children; life was pretty rocky and scary at that point. We rented five houses in 3 years. Paying rent was a massive blow to us. We often wondered where we went wrong, should we move back, should we give up on our dreams, living paycheck to paycheck, and it just looked and felt as though we were getting nowhere. For the next four years in Mudgee, it was darn tough, we had no family close, and we had no real friends at that point.

Now, this is the best part. Fast forward to today, we own a 50-acre farm, our family is now three kids, two girls and one boy. My husband and myself have worked, and I have studied darn hard for the last five years. I ran my own Air Bnb business in the heart of Mudgee. I also ran my own cleaning services. From there, I ventured out. I always wanted to do something to help others and to inspire others, so I started studying Bowen Therapy. Bowen works with our mind, body and soul. I love the fact that I can help so many people in all walks of life. As you have read, life hasn't always been easy. It has been tough, it has been fun, but most importantly, it has been a lesson every step of the way.

I read and listen to audio books and podcasts about personal development every day. When I have the opportunity, I love going to live personal development weekends, mainly these are held in the city. I am working on myself to be a better mother, wife, christian and businesswoman every single day. As a successful businesswoman, it hasn't always been easy. Like I said earlier, I have always felt as though I needed to work harder than the person beside me. Maybe that is because I doubt my worth at times. It is not easy. There will be times you don't believe in yourself, there will be times you want to give up and wonder why you started, there will be times when family, friends and people you don't even know judge you, think they know better, give you their advice, but I can tell you one thing, it's darn worth all the hard work!

I'm actually writing this chapter sitting on the river banks of the Bogan river in NSW with my family. From here, we are taking off to broken hill, down to the Murray river, and from there, making our way back home via the beautiful coast with an easy time frame. Blessed and so grateful is an understatement. I have the freedom to travel this beautiful country. I have the freedom to help others. Every day I feel blessed. I am so grateful for every day I get to spend with my family, friends and loved ones.

WHY

If we talk about a WHY- What is your WHY? - What is my WHY? This is such a serious and hot topic in our home.

What is my WHY? Why do I push myself? Why do I get out of bed in the morning? Why do I keep going? What do I want?

We have a one year plan, a five-year plan and a 10-year plan. My why, my goals and what keeps me going. For myself, that's an easy question. My Why - Is my family and to inspire and help as many people as I can. Having three young children, I feel as though it is so important for me to show them that dreams can come true. If we work towards our goals, we can achieve them if we have a plan in place. I like to call it our "Fair Dinkum Plan", a plan that makes sense, a plan that we can achieve with hard work and a plan that is going to push our limits and be worth every trial along the way. We all need a why. Why do you get out of bed in the morning? Why do you do what you do? So maybe ask yourself what is your WHY? What keeps you going? What gets you excited!?

Happiness, another topic we often speak freely about in our home. Does it make you happy? I have been in some dark, unhappy places with work and lifestyle, and I know now if it is not making me happy, if it is making me dread getting out of bed, I need to sit down and question myself, what can I do to make it better, how can I become happy again, but most importantly how did I get unhappy, and how can I get out of that rut?! Don't get stuck in that awful rut. Think about your happiness. For myself, I know when I'm not happy that, my family suffers too. I get moody, cranky and everything in between. Find your happiness and your Why. A great bit of advice that was given to me at a personal development weekend was this simple but powerful message. You are the people you spend most of your time with. You are what they are; we bounce off one another. I know for myself if I am exposed to negative, unhappy people, my mood changes, my thoughts change, and for myself, I know it is not a good change.

I got where I am today because I worked on myself, my marriage, and my family every day. I have accepted my past and use my past as a beautiful reminder that things will always work out. I knew my weaknesses, I knew what I needed to improve, and I worked hard on those areas. Running two very successful Air Bnbs, running my own cleaning services at the same time took massive hours, having staff and all the behind-the-scenes was tough! But if I didn't do it, if I didn't have my goals, plans, and my WHY, I know I wouldn't be sitting on this beautiful river bank today with no stress because I worked those long hours, I had my WHY clear from taking our first step into our new world of moving away from our families and work. I had a very clear vision. I knew I wanted to do something to help and inspire others. Having these two businesses has allowed me to study Bowen Therapy and get my business up and running. I couldn't be more grateful for that! To become a Bowen therapist has taken many hours of practical work, log-book hours, and so many hours that turned into day and months of theory work. I love what I do. I love knowing I can help others, whether it be physical help or mental help. I have people open up to me and trust me daily with their stories, trauma, sexually assaulted victims, physical pain, mental health, and so much more. For me, Bowen therapy is so much more than just a treatment. I have one lady that comes to see me every week to just be able to sleep for 1 hour, uninterrupted sleep, no children with her, no stress of work, no stress of home duties and the list doesn't stop. I do the Bowen treatment on this lady, and she sleeps. For many, this wouldn't mean much, but imagine switching off for 1 hour. When life gets crazy, we tend to brush it under the mat, tend to think it is normal, that if we are not stressed, if we are not working our bums off and getting nowhere, it's totally normal, but it's totally NOT NORMAL!

My goal is to help all kinds of women to be a shoulder to lean on to be a safe haven to show them they are strong and loved. In a world where we are always so busy, so stressed and always have 100 things on our minds. This treatment has allowed me to use Bowen to help open up and heal women of all walks of life, mentally and physically. I will travel Australia, our beautiful country, taking my hands, ears and my heart with me and one treatment at a time to help many women.

About the Author

From leaving school in year 9 to now owning and operating her own very successful Bowen therapy business.

Rachael helps women in all walks of life, from sexually abused victims, child abused victims, women that need physical help and works with women helping heal them via their mind, body and soul.

Rachael lives in Country NSW on a beautiful farm. When Rachael isn't helping local women she is travelling with her husband and her young family and is often found helping women where they are on holidays or travelling through towns.

Email: rachaelsbowentherapy@gmail.com
Instagram:
www.instagram.com/rach.hall91/?igshid=YmMyMTA2M2Y%3D

Susan Kommor

From Grief to Gratitude

I saved the cake plate!

I hugged it tightly in my arms as I watched the men remove everything else that was left in the house....

That is not an image I projected growing up in Long Island, New York.

FLASHBACK:

As a young teenager of 15 years old, I was in my happy place, with my sweet family in our joyful home, when my world suddenly turned upside down.

Life as I knew it, with my caring Mom & Dad and my two awesome brothers, would be drastically altered forever.

I would learn what it's like to deal with grief, with the untimely death of my beloved father at age 46.

My Dad was a former engineer turned entrepreneur. In the

short time, he was with us, besides being a fabulous Dad, he created computer schools in the 60s, which became a global franchise; he purchased a bank in an auction, created new branding, and expanded to 2 more branches; and he made his way to Wall Street by starting a municipal bond brokerage business.

He was a visionary, a thinker, a reader, and an investor with a keen eye for market trends.

He taught all of us that anything is possible.

Entrepreneurship is in my DNA.

Grief does have the power to tear families apart. My family did the opposite- we became a very close and loving unit.

I tribute that to my Mom, who was my ultimate role model of love and resilience.

Strong women create strong women.

I watched my Mom help us all move forward through the grief, and show us how it's possible to find joy in life, reinvent yourself after loss, and inspire others with an optimistic perspective.

My Mom had a unique way of looking at dire situations and seeing the funny side. We found this to be the thread that kept our little family unit optimistic and close together.

We watched our Mom, who already was an incredible cook, attend Culinary School and become a caterer. When she decided being on her feet all day was no longer viable, she took a job in the accounting department of a big food company- Entenmann's (we enjoyed the fringe benefits of boxes of chocolate fudge cakes and chocolate chip cookies that she brought home!).

Just like my Mom, I learned when adversity hits, when you get knocked down, you get up and move forward with an optimistic attitude. Believe that everything has a way of working out.

We all stayed close, even though we lived in different states- Mom in New York, one brother in New Jersey, and one brother in California- seeing each other on holidays and in between as much as possible.

After graduating college with a degree in Psychology and Business, I moved to upstate New York with my former husband, where we purchased our first house and where I began a lifelong career in financial services.

I successfully worked up the ladder at Citibank to a Sales Officer position.

I gave birth to two vivacious and joyous daughters. Desiring to have more time at home with them, I successfully persuaded the Citibank officials that I could work 30 hours and get the job done more efficiently and effectively than working the full 40 hours.

I had a signed document allowing me to be a part-time Sales Officer-a major feat at that time.

I held the vision that I could do good work while spending more time with my girls. My girls have always been a priority in my life. Being a Mom is my number one job. When you take the time to understand what is truly important to you, you become resourceful.

We moved back to Long Island when their father finished his internship. I was ecstatic to be back near my family!

I found employment as a Sales Representative for a Parent magazine, happily working from home, where I watched my daughters blossom into talented, brilliant, and loving young girls.

When their father accepted a job in Louisville, Kentucky, I felt uprooted from our lovely neighborhood, from our beautiful house with a pool, a fishpond, a vegetable garden I created, and far away from my family and my Mom.

Our move to Louisville was jolting, but I learned to stay optimistic, and be excited for new adventures. I had completed coursework to become a Certified Financial Planner, so I started looking for financial advisor positions when I inadvertently stumbled on an opportunity to be a youth director at the JCC (Jewish Community Center).

Mom always said to take every opportunity, so I did- thinking it would be a "temporary" one. As it turned out, the "temporary" job soon became permanent. I loved creating events during the year and being camp director in the summer. My girls came off the bus from school right to the JCC, where I had my office in the Teen lounge. They came on trips with me and attended all the events with me. I kept pace with current music trends and even learned how to shoot pool in the Teen lounge! I also embraced the world of fitness and running and successfully completed two mini-marathons.

I was reinventing myself and feeling great, so I did not see it coming….but it did.

Their father moved to Florida to start a new life. I was left as a single Mom in a town that I was beginning to understand and enjoy and where my two daughters were starting to create circles of friends and opportunities.

Divorce was something I never imagined or considered.

My inclination was to run back to NY, but I did not want to uproot and disrupt the lives of my daughters again, so I stayed the course.

Now I needed to find an attorney. And a therapist. But not necessarily in that order.

The divorce proceedings seemed to start an avalanche of unforeseen events. Not only was I going through a learning curve around the legalities of divorce, which went on for years and took me in and out of court, but I also was left to vacate the marital home- which entailed looking through 20 years of belongings and memories.

When the closing date was accelerated, so was the time I had to empty the house. I found myself on my hands and knees flinging things into boxes the day before closing when the buyer's realtor stopped by to do a walk-through. "How will you finish clearing all this out by tomorrow?" she asked. Great question.

I was visibly distraught, so the realtor helped me out by calling a service that would remove all remaining items from the house. It was traumatic to see everything from our basement being hauled out by 3 men into a truck!

I did manage to salvage my Mom's glass cake plate before it was thrown into the abyss.

I saved the cake plate!

I hugged it tightly in my arms as I watched the men from 1-800-Got-Junk, remove everything else in the house.

And we had nowhere to go...

Fortunately, a rental home became available from our realtor. It was a comfortable house in a suburb. The monthly cost was high, with extra pet charges, but I had no other options.

We made it work.

In the meantime, I was dealing with bills and lack of funds to pay them, keeping the lights and water on, and maintaining a household of 2 daughters, a chocolate labrador, 2 cats, and 40 cichlids.

How I ended up with the dog, cats, and all the fish is a bigger conversation.

Life was loving but not always easy. My daughters and I stuck together during the many ups and downs of a single Mom household. We all shared those necessary responsibilities to keep things copacetic in the midst of the chaos. There would be two more house moves and navigating through the labyrinth of the Jefferson County Public School system.

And all those heart-wrenching moments at the airport as I watched my young girls being escorted away from me as "unaccompanied minors" on the plane to fly to Florida to fulfil visitation requirements.

Our cichlids did not survive an ice storm that left us with no electricity for a week. And we would eventually experience the pain of the loss of our cherished pets many years later.

Behind the scenes, I was going through negotiations, subpoenas, making big decisions, and facing all those yellow envelopes I received in the mail that ordered me to appear in court.

I continued to focus on and improve my new role as "Head of Household". We continued to work together as a team and took care of each other. I stayed involved in school events and was committed to keeping the love and laughter going in the household.

With the support of my Mom and my brothers, I moved forward through this intensely challenging season of my life. My incredibly supportive family got me through this situation in a way that I could not imagine without them. I am so grateful.

Shortly afterwards, as we adjusted to our new lifestyle, I was downsized at my job at the JCC.

I was now unemployed.

Time to pivot. Again. Time to take action, to move forward

once again after loss. Through the grief. With an optimistic attitude.

I was offered a Financial Planner position, taking me down the path of my own financial success as I helped others create financial strategies. Working one on one to solve problems and transform lives was extremely fulfilling. I was thrilled to be back in the financial world.

Even more important, I had a flexible schedule. I would set appointments and meet with clients and still attend every field hockey game, choir concert, and school event. I even managed to be at every performance of the Louisville Ballet's Nutcracker that my youngest daughter performed in, with the exception of one that was a private showing for Brown-Forman employees only. Although I admit I did attempt to sneak in!

My daughters are what kept me going. They are in the heart and soul of everything I do. They have inspired me to create a legacy that will help women for generations navigate through loss with divorce.

Strong women create strong women.

Fast forward to now, I am watching my daughters become amazing and inspiring women, thriving as they climb to the top of their companies, achieving their own accolades, marrying remarkable spouses, and creating their own happy households.

During my reign as a financial planner, I was drawn to women going through divorce and became trained in Collaborative Divorce, which is divorce without court. Many decisions are made during the most emotional moments of life, and I wanted to be part of a better way to maneuver the divorce process.

As much as I enjoyed my Financial Planning practice, I found it necessary to leave the corporate arena, so I could offer more products to my clients. I decided to collaborate with a partner in a privately owned financial planning business.

The decision was sound. However, the timing could have been better. It was 2008.

And then came the global financial crisis. Everything came tumbling down, including my partnership and my business.

Now what? Time to pivot. Again.

I remained optimistic through yet another loss and all the fear that comes with it.

At this time, my eldest daughter was in College at University of Central Florida, and my youngest was about to graduate High School and was planning to attend Brandeis University in Massachusetts the following year.

I invested in a financial coaching program with David Bach after reading his book, "Smart Women Finish Rich", with the expectation of becoming one of their financial coaches.

I was determined to leave Kentucky and all the trauma and drama behind me.

I did not foresee that my entire life trajectory was about to change.

At exactly the right moment.

I was introduced to a service that would give me access to an entire law firm without billable hours. I was intrigued. And surprised and maybe a little bit annoyed that I never knew about this service before. With this service, I could talk to an attorney on any area of law, on any issue, get guidance on my rights and options, and not get a bill! It was unbelievable to me that this existed.

I got it, used it, and it worked. As Head of Household, I was no longer alone. I could make better decisions for my family, get guidance, know my options and my rights in any situation.

It was direct sales, and I became an independent business partner of the company so I could offer these services to others. I wanted everyone to have this affordable, legal access- especially women in their new role of Head of Household.

This company also had an entire personal development component, which I embraced.

I was now part of a community of successful entrepreneurs who were already making 6 figure incomes working from home, using a system that I learned and shared with others.

I was building a team of business professionals who would help me spread the word of this service to their clients and colleagues. I was starting my journey of building my own home-based business using this same system while simultaneously uncovering my own true worth, value, and potential.

I have since been on a life-altering journey into my own self and the power of my own mind. It was during this time that I learned the teachings of Abraham-HIcks, the law of attraction, and the power of gratitude. I learned that thoughts are things.

At about that same time, my now husband, Steve, entered my life. I knew we were meant to be together on our first date. We would connect the dots later to unfold the perfect sequence of events and circumstances that brought us together. We were meant for each other all along. I finally uncovered the real reason why I was in Kentucky- I would find my soulmate here- my perfect match.

We have a wonderful marriage where joy, pleasure, respect,

devotion, admiration, and true love is always present. I am so grateful to have someone who allows me to grow and who believes in me. Our love and devotion to each other gets better every day. We are happier, wealthier, and healthier than we have ever been before.

I was at the beginning of what would be my mission- to impact and transform the lives of other professional Moms going through divorce and to guide them as they take on the role of Head of Household, take charge of their financial future, and raise strong and confident children.

I went from broken, broke, and downsized out of a job, to building a 6 figure business of my own, working from home, and inspiring and empowering entrepreneurs nationwide to transform their lives through my services and my coaching.

Grief would enter my life again in a big way in 2018, which brought about an almost unbearable loss of all our parents in that same year- my father-in-law in January, my mother-in-law in June, and then my Mom in October.

Finding meaning in the loss, and moving forward through the grief, led me to deep work with grief expert David Kessler. I have since become a Certified Grief Educator to grow myself and also to better serve my clients.

My personal life strategy is to continue to nurture my

relationship with my husband, Steve, to inspire others that you absolutely can find your soulmate and perfect love later in life; to support and empower my community with my time and my services; and to continue my commitment and dedication to being a devoted Mom and role model for my daughters. Extraordinary success is achievable when you focus on what's possible and not on your past circumstances.

I am committed to getting better every day. I continue to do intense work on my mindset and limiting beliefs. I discovered that I could not do this work alone, and invested in Coaches, Mastermind programs, and Inner Circles with other like-minded entrepreneurs to continually get better, inspire others, and make an impact.

I am on a mission to educate and empower women to rise above outdated beliefs that create limitations based on age and to elevate their lives and businesses to the next level while navigating through loss.

Are you a professional woman experiencing any or all of these: broken, broke, raising children as a single Mom, downsized from a job, or considering working or building your own business from home?

If so, you are not alone. Let's connect and have a conversation- if you are ready to move forward.

If you are going through or have gone through this process of divorce, it's important to understand and address the loss. The death of a marriage is a real loss.

Grief stays with us, but we can move forward with the grief. Grief must be witnessed.

As a Certified Grief Educator, I can help you move through grief. With divorce loss, we have secondary losses and possible traumatic grief.

When we work together, I help you move through David Kessler's six needs of the grieving, which I refigured to create the acronym: "WE RISE"

1. To Have Your Pain **Witnessed**   W
2. To **Express** Your Feelings   E
3. To **Release** The Burden of Guilt   R
4. To **Integrate** the Pain and the Love   I
5. To **Set** you Free of Old Wounds   S
6. To **Enjoy** Meaning in Life After Loss   E

Are you ready to take control of your life? To own your future?

Unstoppable!

Together, WE RISE!

You are not alone.

I can help you work through the grief, and provide the financial & legal support that will empower you to create the life you desire.

I'm rooting for you!

xox Susan

"Your mess does not disqualify you from making your dream come true." ~ Ed Mylett

About the Author

A former Certified Financial Planner turned entrepreneur, Susan Kommor Is a Coach & Certified Grief Educator, providing guidance & tools for women going through divorce: to help manage the conflict, to address the emotions of grief, and to handle the financial and legal issues that ensue. Susan has over 30 years of experience in the financial services industry.

Born and raised in New York, Susan has called Louisville, Kentucky, home for over 20 years. Susan is happily married to Steve Kommor and is COO of their family-owned business, Cherokee Coins & Jewelry. Susan is currently collaborating to create a guide for women going through divorce- a step-by-step blueprint of how to move forward. Connect with Susan to be added to the waitlist for upcoming book announcements.

Email: susan@susankommor.com
Website: www.susankommor.com
Instagram: www.instagram.com/susanpackkommor

Suz Tutty

Raise your right hand if you're a coffee drinker, and if you don't drink coffee, raise your left hand. Now, sit back and relax with a cuppa of your choice…

I'm Suz, the CEO and founder of Irresistible and Co., whose mission is to empower women to Become Irresistible with Confidence. I'm very fortunate that every day I get to work with women who want to ooze confidence and radiate happiness from within - more on this later; let me give you an insight into my life and why I now do what I do.

A little bit about me - who am I, and where do I come from? I'm Irish, born and raised, and come from the most picturesque village called Hollywood, Co. Wicklow. Fun fact: it's where Hollywood in LA got its name from, and YES, we even have a Hollywood sign which was made by my dad in 1998 when the Tour de France passed through our little cul-de-sac village. I'm the youngest of 3 girls and have the most amazing parents. Our family is well-known in our community, so that paved and shaped my upbringing significantly.

Growing up, I was a reticent and well-behaved girl - always wanting to do well and make my parents proud - I thrived on validation from my parents, particularly my dad, because I didn't know how to self-validate myself. I endured bullying throughout primary and secondary school, and it was always brushed under the carpet because that's how things were dealt with in a rural Catholic village in Ireland.

As I entered my teen years, I started dating, and my choice of males was less than desirable because I chose many partners who, let's say politely, didn't know how to treat young women. At this stage of my life, I never knew how to speak up for myself, so I tolerated poor behaviour - because I wanted to be liked. This was not a very healthy way of dealing with issues, and as time progressed. When I went through breakups, they were devastating, the heartbreak unbearable, which led to significant levels of rejection.

As time passed, I ended up at Uni, had a boyfriend and joined the student movement; this was where my journey of being a voice for others started. I started to surround myself with like-minded people who wanted to challenge policies within our Uni and at the Government level. Within a year, I was the voice for over 4,000 full and part-time students - I thrived in this environment. Upon completing Uni, I represented students at a national level and was an officer for 10 Universities within Leinster. At this stage, I was long-distance with my boyfriend, who moved to Perth in 2010; we were long-distance for 18 months.

In April 2012, I finally moved to Perth, which was a rollercoaster ride from doing regional work of washing lettuce to becoming a Sales Manager for Fitness First. Working for Fitness First instilled my love for helping others with their health and fitness. It also instilled in me the fundamentals of understanding sales and how each interaction is a sale or traction of some sort.

Life at this stage was great - I was in a job I loved, although it was fueled by anxiety, and I had a boyfriend, who soon became my fiance in 2013. Wedding planning commenced, and the big day was secured for Friday, 31 July 2015 - a 3-day event. It really was one of the best days of my life - I was surrounded by my nearest and dearest. Life was bliss; newlywed and travelling around Ireland with my husband; what more could I ask for?

As our time in Ireland came to an end, it was time to pack our bags and return to the land down under. We slotted back into Perth live, and by Christmas, we were both working FIFO on a 4/1 swing with one day off. This was probably the most challenging job I've ever had - a pasty Irish gal, working in the Pilbara, 40-degree days, flies and not to mention the 40-plus rooms to clean! As time passed, I moved into the kitchen - finally in continuous A/C. During this time, my life changed significantly, and it was the beginning of the end of my marriage. It was devastating, and I had taken on the persona of someone I wasn't; I became unrecognisable, and that version of me caused so much pain and hurt to my loved ones.

By April 2017, my marriage was over; I walked away to pursue a relationship built on fantasy and everything that wasn't going well in my marriage. It was like something you'd see in a movie. It was an emotional rollercoaster, and it has now become one of my greatest lessons! For a significant amount of time after all of this, I was experiencing significant mental health issues due to being pulled in several directions and trying to please everyone else except myself. As the days and weeks passed, I did not know who I was. If you asked me the difference between right and wrong, I didn't know which. This period of time is something I'm not proud of, however, I also know that there are many reasons this chapter of my life came crashing down.

Now, why did I choose this avenue of Empowerment Coaching? Well, strap in because I'm going to take you on a journey - let's rewind to 2019, which was a pivotal year in re-shaping my character. Wow, it's almost been four years since I started this journey of self-discovery.

2019, a year where I was hours away from committing suicide, fell out with my dad, and ended a toxic relationship that was predominately psychological abuse; however, it also included much more than you care to imagine! Think Tinder Swindler without the luxury & that is no exaggeration; I even had the watch situation. I had a fibroid removed and changed the belief that I was not enough; I thought the world would be better off without me that year to embracing a new belief that I am enough. I'm sharing this with you because I want you to know that you have the power to choose your destiny. We all will have "life" happen to us; it's how we choose to navigate it that is our superpower.

It was not a pleasant time in my life; even as I write this chapter, it is hard to comprehend the life I was living in 2019, a life based around people-pleasing, being dishonest and most of all, living my life based around a victim mentality.

It was 31 May 2019, a Friday night I remember so vividly. I was ready to leave this world; I had had enough of the life I was living - suicide seemed like the easy way out, and it would all be over. As I was driving to the coast in Perth, I was ready to leave this world. I had sent a goodbye email to my then-husband (no, this wasn't a toxic relationship), and he had forwarded it to my parents back in Ireland. Between them and another one or two friends, I had constant calls, which I chose to ignore. As I was driving along Great Eastern Highway, I asked myself, "what are you doing?". I turned my car around and, at that moment, decided that suicide wasn't the way to solve this - I had to take extreme ownership and responsibility for my actions, which at times were very toxic and deceitful.

Looking back, I never wanted to commit suicide; it was a cry for help; I had lost myself and felt like Humpty dumpty splattered all over the ground - my life had crumbled all around me. I had severed the relationship with my parents, lost a marriage, and was a shell of my former self - completely and utterly lost. Thankfully, I had an amazing psychologist - when I first met her, she thought I was bipolar and had a personality disorder. It turned out I was just a high-functioning, anxious person - it explained so much.

As 2019 progressed, I had a fibroid removed - this was an energetic cord, and once it was released, it changed my trajectory. I was very slowly starting to reconnect with my gut and intuition. Thankfully, this changed everything for me, and it's when I started to take my power back, and it allowed me to begin re-discovering who I was.

After attending a 3 Day personal development seminar in October, I went from "I'm not enough" to "I am Enough". It was the first time I started saying yes to myself. I resigned from my job in blue-collar recruitment on Tuesday, two days after the three-day event and three weeks later, I was in Hawaii delving deeper into finding out who I was. This was when I started living my true authentic life.

Don't get me wrong; it hasn't been easy. However, I wouldn't change the journey for love or money because, without the life-changing moments of 2019, I wouldn't be where I am today.

When I returned from Hawaii, I had found my purpose - I wanted to help people overcome their limiting beliefs and live their true authentic life. This was the beginning of my career in the Coaching Space, and boy, it opened me to a whole new world!

I spent two and a half years working with a fantastic organisation where I was privileged to coach over 4,500 to overcome their limiting beliefs and start living their true authentic life. During this time, I also supported new coaches in establishing their own Coaching Businesses. I was so fortunate to impact the lives of so many worldwide - seeing them succeed was the greatest reward I could have asked for. Empowering women to stand in their power, which is a very vulnerable thing to do, gave me so much joy - even when they tried to talk themselves out of starting their own businesses. One of my most extraordinary testimonies is the amazing Elsa Morgan. Being able to support her almost two years ago and seeing the platform she has created to impact women worldwide is phenomenal.

In July 2022, I formally launched Irresistible & Co. it was time for me to fly the safety net and step into the entrepreneurial world. And what a journey that has been! Stories like Elsa's have encouraged me to step into my power and surrender my higher self to serving women who have gone through their journeys to Become Irresistible in their own right.

Having coached women to step into their power and start their businesses, I was now that woman. It's certainly not an easy journey to establish your own business, especially when building a personal brand. By doing this, I'm now opening myself and my entire life to the public eye and with that comes the good opinion of others (which you might call judgement)! It also brings my past into question - some of which I can't fully disclose.

My purpose is to use my life experiences to help others through their darkest days and help women find the light at the end of the tunnel. You see, we all have our belief system, and it is this system that can hold us back from reaching our full potential. I can say this wholeheartedly, as I've been going through this since starting my own business. Why would she work with me? I'm not good enough or deserving enough to do this. The list of questions like this is endless. However, I can tell you that if I can shift this, you can turn this. If I had believed all of my limiting beliefs, I'd have thrown the towel weeks, even months ago. Thankfully I haven't, and that is why you're reading this.

I know my purpose is far greater than I even realise; I can impact lives far and wide through storytelling, sharing my journey and coaching women to Become Irresistible with

Confidence. My mission is to encourage the women of today to step into their power, ooze confidence, and radiate happiness. When you are "irresistible", you will shine from within, walk with your head held high, and have this glow that everyone will want. When someone stops you in the street and asks you what you've been doing because you look terrific, you will tell them that you are irresistible.

You will be a walking advocate for something that we all have within, the power and ability to become irresistible by oozing confidence and radiating happiness from within. It's like the golden ticket from Charlie and the Chocolate Factory.

How do you Become Irresistible, you ask? It's straightforward. It requires you to go deep within, to dream about the life you desire and want to create without judgement or limitation. It requires you to audit your social circles, social media and the environments you place yourself in. You have a choice - you can continue to live the life that you're living and settle for "basic", or you can challenge yourself to create a life you wish to jump out of bed for in the mornings. It all comes down to you. For every choice you make, there's a choice you don't, and for every decision you make, there's a decision you don't - there's no right or wrong, just outcome.

I have created a 10 Step Process that empowers women to develop a self-fulling life through Becoming Irresistible with C-O-N-F-I-D-E-N-C-E. Through this process, my mission is to impact each woman I encounter and to ensure that I leave them feeling inspired and empowered after connecting with me.

C - Clarity of Thoughts: This is where you will develop a clear understanding of your values, beliefs, and strengths

O - Own your Strengths: Together, we will emphasise your unique qualities and abilities

N - Nurture a Positive Mindset: Implementing practising gratitude, focusing on the present moment, and surrounding yourself with positive people

F - Flexibility: Creating a flexible life allowing you to be open to change and adapt to new situations

I - Inner Voice: Learning to listen and trust your inner voice, feeling into your intuition and communicating with clarity and certainty

D - Decision Making: Developing the ability to make decisions effectively

E - Embrace Vulnerability: Being open to learning from your mistakes and being comfortable with uncertainty

N - Networking: Build a support system of positive people and mentors who are moving you forward

C - Consistency: Stay consistent in your actions and efforts in life

E - Empowerment: Empowering yourself and taking control of your life

Having a process will help you navigate your next steps, and this will help you create a plan to design your irresistible life.

Some of this may or may not have resonated with you, and some may have even triggered you. You might even decide that I'm not your cup of tea and guess what - that's completely okay. Whatever your opinion of me now that I've let you into my life and shared, what has shaped my character and business is not my business. I am merely a mirror for you. When we see something in others, good or bad, ask yourself what is that showing within me - is it a positive or negative emotion? Either way, dig deep and feel into it because it's time to heal yourself so you, too, can Become Irresistible.

This is just the beginning of Irresistible & Co., and my mission is to empower women like you to Become Irresistible. So, I ask you, what will your Irresistible life look like?

> *"Confidence makes us beautiful, and it comes from accepting yourself. The moment you accept yourself, it makes everything better."~ Dianne Von Furstenberg, The Woman I wanted to be*

About the Author

For the last decade, Suz Tutty's life has been a journey outward and inward.

First, she moved from Hollywood, Co. Wicklow, Ireland, to Perth, Western Australia, in 2012. Her move led to many new experiences, which she outlines in this guide.

Then, she embarked on a spiritual journey after discovering how connecting to her higher-self, allowed her to open her own Pandora's Box, which was the starting point of a new chapter in her life.

Third, she began a personal development journey in 2019. She loved what she learned so much; she felt inspired to help others. She persuaded her then-mentor to allow her to impact the lives of others within his global organisation.

Since then, her enthusiasm for impacting people's lives has only grown. She has committed to raising mental health awareness to eliminate the taboo associated with talking about emotions and feelings.

If you're excited about starting your journey, the next step is to get in touch with Suz Tutty of Irresistible & Co. Together; you can identify the best fit for you!

Facebook: www.facebook.com/SuzTutts
Instagram: www.instagram.com/suztuttyempowermentcoach

Terri-Lynn Chaplin

From grief to serving & impacting the world

I quickly turned my head and looked again. Since my son Tyler's accident, I find myself doing that often – looking again. I glanced out the front window of our home and thought I saw his car parked on the curb. Out of the corner of my eye, I could have sworn I saw him walking up the driveway toward the front door, but when my thoughts turned back to reality, I realized I was looking at a butterfly dancing playfully in the flower garden. I inhaled deeply, and as I slowly exhaled, all the moments of joy, pain, love, laughter, and loss released from within me just as the butterfly took flight in a blur of color.

Deep avoidance – that's where my mind was on this particular morning. The time was fast approaching when I would see my son's lifeless body for the first time since his accident. The beating of my heart was so loud that it was impossible to focus on even the smallest of tasks. I was numb, in denial, and afraid that I might not awaken from this nightmare in which I was suddenly the main character. My eyes were swollen, and they physically hurt each time I reached up to wipe away the steady flow of tears. I missed my son so much, and each day brought with it another realization of something we would never experience together. All the things we take for granted as parents – college graduation, his first love, buying his first house, getting married, becoming a father – all had been stripped from me. The injustice of being cheated out of my role as a mother and my son's life being cut short was devastating. I had never felt more helpless in my life.

Walking towards the front of the room, each step bringing me closer to him, I found it an exhausting task. "This is just a dream," ran through my mind continuously, and then there I was. That first sight was gut-wrenching and left me devoid of breath. He appeared as if he was merely sleeping peacefully, but the realizations were coming at me with a propelling force – I would never again see his face, stroke his hair, hear his voice, or receive one of his amazing hugs. As a parent, what do you do with that? How do you process that?

"I wish I could fast forward a year because I don't know what to do with the turmoil inside of me," I said to Del as we clung to each other for support.

The small cut above his left ear caught my attention first, and my initial reaction was to hold and protect him. A mother's love is fierce and nurturing, and at that moment, those instincts took control, only this time, I couldn't fix it, and that was heartbreaking. The guilt threatened to consume me – was he scared during his accident? Did he call out for me? He was completely alone, terrified, and needed me, and I wasn't there for him. As I stood there, running my fingers through his hair, a flood of memories was racing through my mind – the day he was born, his first tooth, his first birthday spent at the zoo, learning to ride a bike, our trip to Aruba together –so many memories kept coming. Del, standing next to me, placed his arm across my shoulders and pulled me into him as I began to cry uncontrollably.

"He looks so handsome in his new suit," I said. I could vividly remember the day he put it on for his first interview. I watched as he walked differently, with confidence – something he hadn't done previously. He was so excited about his future.

Unable to move from his side, I continued stroking his hair and remembering him as a little boy, and that's when it happened – something awe-inspiring, almost magical, that triggered a shift inside of me like a physical force. It was no subtle feeling but can only be described as a shove reminiscent of a tidal surge slamming against my body. Whatever it was, there was no doubt that it was meant to grab my attention. I found myself contemplating the idea that there was something more, something beyond this world that we live in. I felt an incessant need for knowledge and understanding about things greater than what we experience here on earth. So many thoughts were whirling through my mind as I stood there, studying his face – so many unique qualities and quirks were hidden behind those eyes. Would all that cease to exist simply because his heart had stopped beating? That is something I would ponder repeatedly in the days, weeks, and months to come.

The first couple weeks after the accident hadn't offered much time for idle thoughts as our home had been a revolving door of friends and family, and were busy with the funeral and celebration of life. And now, suddenly, there I was, sitting alone in the empty house, consumed with despair. Losing a child is unimaginable – it tests your every belief and your optimism in the world. The silence was deafening, and it was then that the sorrow and anguish could no longer be ignored. Sitting at Tyler's desk, staring out the window of his bedroom, I began to scream so loud and so violently, "This isn't fair! Why did you take my child?"

There I was, with a deep void in my life, yet everyone around me continued with their life as if nothing happened. The one person who had been a constant in my life for the past eighteen years was gone – never to tousle my hair again, never to hug me or say, "I love you, Mom" again. So many shattered dreams. An unrealized future just gone. I was suffering the worst loss of my life, the most unbearable emotional pain and all my friends and family were at work, having lunch with friends, making dinner for their families, and continuing with their day-to-day lives. Didn't they know that I was hurting? Didn't they care that I was left with a tremendous void in my life? It was during those days that I didn't know how I would ever smile again – how I would ever allow myself to feel joy again. The feelings of injustice and profound grief threatened to end the happy life that I knew just as quickly as Tyler's life had ended.

I wasn't even sure how to exist or allow others to see my pain. For months I got up each day, put on my "grief mask," and pretended that everything was okay, and for the most part, that worked with the exception of Del - there was no hiding from him. My constant supporter, he encouraged me to talk about my feelings and offered a safe space in which to do that. One evening while we were sitting together at the dinner table, Del reached over and took my hand in his.

"What's going on? I can see it in your eyes that there's so much you aren't saying."

"Nothing," I muttered while wanting to scream, "My son died, that's what's going on," but I knew he was only asking out of concern.

"Terri Lynn, you know that I know you. Please talk to me," he encouraged.

As the tears began to pour from my eyes, all I could say was "thank you" as we stood clinging to each other in a moment of shared anguish. I had come to rely on him so much and soon found that in the comfort of his arms, I could escape the pain inside my heart, even if only for a moment.

A few days later, while getting my haircut, my friend and hairstylist shared with me the specifics of an encounter she had with a local psychic medium. After listening to the details, my interest was piqued to the point that I decided to forgo my skepticism and find out for myself. In contemplating what this could mean for my life, I knew that if real, a visit such as the one she described could completely change the trajectory of my grief. Considering that, I proceeded to make an appointment utilizing a fictitious name and email address so that I could eliminate the possibility that she would have read one of the many articles written about Tyler. I knew that I couldn't have any doubt if this were to create real, true change within me.

The day had arrived, and I was feeling a mix of emotions – apprehension, anxiety, hesitation, and excitement, to name a few. As always, Del was right by my side. As we entered the office and took a seat, I could feel my stomach churning and found it difficult to quiet my mind of all the "what ifs".

"What if we discover that we can still communicate with Tyler?" I asked Del.

"That would be a blessing," he replied, gently rubbing my back.

"I don't know what I would do without you here. I am so grateful for you," I told him.

"There's nowhere I'd rather be," he said, smiling.

The moment the door opened, and Natalie stepped into the waiting area, a sense of calm washed over me. A very pretty lady, she had kind eyes and a warmness about her that instantly eased my anxiety. Leading us into an adjacent room, Natalie took a seat on one side of the room and motioned for us to sit on the couch directly across from her.

"Did you bring a photo of your loved one, as we discussed?" she asked. As I reached to hand her Tyler's senior portrait, she asked, "and what is his name?"

"His name is Tyler," I said while noticing an obvious shift in her demeanor.

"I must be completely honest with you. I recognize the picture and his name from recent stories that I have seen on television and the local news sites. I don't know all the details, but I just want you to know that I am familiar with it," she said.

"Thank you for your honesty," Del said, squeezing my hand reassuringly.

The room grew quiet as Natalie lowered her head and began to slowly run her hand across Tyler's picture.

"Alright, so I'm just picking up on the energy of him right now, and so it helps me if I just put it out there so you can tell me if it feels like him or not. I saw him doing these moves like he was – I don't know how to say it – he was kind of vivacious, not dancing around but sort of. I don't know if that's any part of his personality. Do you know what I'm saying? I can see him like scooching down. Does that make sense?" she asked, giggling out loud.

She was describing perfectly how he used to knock on our bedroom door, and when I would open it, he would crouch down and do a little dance while saying, "I love you, Uugie." As she spoke, goosebumps began to form on my scalp and work their way down the rest of my body. The feeling was indescribable as the tears began to seep from within and slide down my cheeks.

"This young man feels like he was excited about his future – this was definitely accidental. He was riding high on life and feeling good about things and being a little too carefree, maybe. I feel like he was just out for a drive. He is showing me that he turned around because of the rain. Does that make sense?"

"Yes, it had been raining, and his tires hydroplaned on the wet pavement."

"He does want you to know he is okay. I see him standing in the doorway of your bedroom. Have you felt him there? He really feels how much you love him. There is somebody there with him – a man wearing a ball cap. Is his father on the other side?"

"Yes," I said as the tears graduated from a seep to an outright pour. The vision of Tyler reuniting with his dad brought with it an eerie sense of peace that would go on to offer me comfort in the years to come.

"It's okay," Del whispered, squeezing my hand reassuringly.

"I don't know what he's referring to, but he says that Del said, 'take your time, take your time,' and he says you were patient with him. You would give him advice, but you didn't push him."

"That's true. Del was very patient with Tyler and would always tell him that he could have anything he wanted in life, but he needed to slow down and take his time," I said.

"He says you're smart, but you had to figure out a lot on your own. He admires that about you. Do you know what he's talking about?" she said to Del.

Del smiled. "Yes, I pretty much taught myself everything I

know about computers, and I spent a lot of time passing that knowledge along to Tyler."

"Do you have anything that you want to ask him?" she asked.

"What about the police department? Does he know how big of a deal they made of him? Did he see his funeral?" asked Del.

"Well, I already know what I know, but I don't recall seeing anything about the funeral specifically, so let me ask him," Natalie replied.

There had not been any coverage of the funeral service inside the funeral home itself, so I felt like her response could truly solidify this experience for me.

"They didn't give him a uniform, did they?" she asked.

"No," we replied in unison.

"I'm trying to get confirmation from him. He shows me this man, and he said the word devastated. I got a middle-aged man with greying hair, and he said this man was devastated. He's showing me some kind of ceremony. He is showing me the man standing at a podium or something, and then he is presenting you with something."

"There was a podium, and no one knew about it, and the Sheriff deputized him," said Del.

"He feels like he was happy in his life. He liked how his life was going – where it was going, and he felt very loved," she added.

I attribute that visit, as being pivotal in altering the path of my grief. To know with 100% certainty that Tyler's spirit continues to be ever-present and to have the confirmation that he was the "higher power" pushing me to learn more offered immense comfort. Somehow the finality of his passing wasn't so final anymore. He hears me when I speak to him, and he shows me signs that he is nearby, and I am forever grateful for that. In providing the push that I needed, Tyler had extended me the gift of serenity and hope, and I have made it my purpose to share that gift with others in his honor.

One of my first undertakings was to craft a goodbye letter to Tyler to include things that had gone unsaid, that which I felt guilty about, all that I loved about him, and how I was forever grateful to have been blessed with being his mom. Putting pen to paper proved to be a monumental undertaking and one that I started and stopped countless times. It wasn't until I had completed the letter and read it aloud that I had a true understanding of its impact and how powerful it was in my healing process. That letter offered me a form of closure that I was desperately searching for, and that was invaluable in my healing process.

I also found it therapeutic to offer support to others who were also mourning the loss of a child, as it provided a sense of purpose. One morning, approximately three years after Tyler's passing, I read the story of a local young man that had been tragically killed in an accident. Carefully reading the words, I was overcome with actual, physical pain for what I knew his parents were experiencing. With the help of social media, I was able to locate his mother and reached out to her via messenger. In the months following his passing, she relied on me as a source of support and reassurance as someone who understood her loss. Eventually, we met in person, along with our husbands, so that we could offer each other a long, overdue hug. To finally meet her and embrace her was transformative for me. That encounter was the beginning of something beautiful as it solidified my "why" and was significant in my decision to become a Certified Master Grief Coach.

They say that knowledge is key, and in my case, educating myself and opening my mind were crucial to processing my grief in a healthy manner and ultimately learning to allow joy to coexist alongside it. I believe that if we allow our hearts and minds to be open to the possibilities and actively listen to our intuition, we can witness the beauty of the signs that our loved ones provide for us. If you are struggling and stuck in grief, here are three things that helped me:

Use mindfulness to become aware of your thoughts and feelings so that you are better prepared to focus your attention on positive things rather than the unconstructive thoughts that come naturally.

Create a gratitude list to serve as a reminder of what you have to be thankful for.

Understand that your grief journey will be unique to you.

My vision for the future is to live my life in gratitude and service to others so that I may have a positive impact on this world. I strive each day to bring awareness to the topic of grief, its meaning, coping mechanisms, and how we can best support others who have experienced a loss or major life change. Through this process, I have learned to cherish all the memories created with my son and to allow my grief to be present alongside pure happiness as I continue to grow and experience all of life's joys. I am creating the life of my dreams and aspire to help others in their quest to do the same.

About the Author

Terri Lynn Chaplin is the founder of TLC Grief Coaching LLC and owner of ZYIA with TLC, Independent Rep. She is a Certified Master Grief Coach and Strategic Life Coaching Practitioner who supports others in their journey for growth and healing.

Terri attributes the loss of her first husband and her son as being the catalyst that drives her to live her life in gratitude and service to others.

Terri is a wife, mother, and mentor to many who enjoys traveling, cooking, and reading for personal development. She currently resides in Tampa, Florida, with her beloved husband, Del, stepson, Sean, and their two rescue dogs, Isabella and Cairo.

Website: www.tlcgriefcoaching.com,
Facebook Group: www.facebook.com/groups/5883978758335502
Facebook page: www.facebook.com/terri.chaplin

Theresa Seitz

Walking away from a successful career... to building a multi-million dollar business

I knew I wanted to work for Walt Disney World from the time I was twelve.

I was one of the lucky ones who knew exactly what I wanted to do with my life. When people would ask me what I wanted to be when I grew up - my response was always the same, "the next Michael Eisner".

A big reason I went to Indiana University was because they partnered with Disney for the Walt Disney World College Program. This is a 6-month program in Orlando where you work in one of Disney's Theme Parks or Resorts and take classes through Disney University. I later learned I was the only applicant that came to the interview in a suit.

In January 1998, my dad and grandfather drove me down to Orlando to drop me off for my College Program. I spent the next month working, networking with leaders, and having the time of my life. Were we paid a lot? Absolutely not. Would I recommend doing the College Program to any college student? Absolutely.

One of the leaders I sat down with was named DJ. Thank goodness DJ had a sense of humor. I was working as a front desk hostess at the Disney Institute (now Disney's Saratoga Springs Resort), and DJ was my front office manager. Essentially, DJ was my boss's boss. When he asked me what my goals were, without thinking, I replied, "I want your job!" He just smiled and put me in touch with a gentleman in Professional Recruitment. DJ recently retired from the company, and his name was put on a window on Main Street, USA, in the Magic Kingdom. This is an honor reserved for very few.

The gentleman he put me in touch with in Professional Recruitment, Jamie, was a great guy. During our meeting, he told me all about a new program called a Management Internship. The name was appropriate - that was exactly what it was. Disney was hiring college kids they thought had potential to be a leader within the company upon graduation. This was also a six-month program.

It just so happened they had an intern who was supposed to come down for the spring program but had a family emergency. I was told the spot was at the Caribbean Beach Resort Front Office and was mine if I wanted it.

Talk about being blown away. I think for the first time in my life, I was truly speechless. I was out of my CP housing, and in a new apartment the very next day I started my Management Internship 2 days later.

The program was fabulous. I learned so incredibly much. I learned I didn't have to know every computer system or the answer to every single question. I had the best team of Cast Members who knew all of that. My biggest takeaway from that program was that if you take care of your employees, they will help you take care of your customers.

As the end of summer approached, I was preparing to return to Bloomington to finish my degree. I checked my email to find a 30 minute meeting request from our General Manager, Manny. Over the time I was there, I had developed a great relationship with Manny, but it's a little nerve-wracking to see a meeting request from your GM, not knowing what it's regarding.

A week later, dressed in my best suit, I went to his office. I didn't realize how scary the words "he's ready for you." can be.

The meeting went beyond my expectations - he offered me a full-time position effective immediately.

"Oh, Manny, I am so honored to be asked to stay. I can't. I have to go back to Bloomington and finish my degree. This is the easiest and hardest decision, but I just can't."

My next thought was, did I just ruin my chances of a long term career with Disney??? Was this the dumbest thing I could do?'

Without missing a beat, Manny got a huge smile on his face and said, "That's my girl. Go back to school. This is what I was hoping you would say. You staying at the resort is what's best for the business. Would we love you to stay? Absolutely. We value you as a leader. Is it what's best for you? I think the best thing you can do is go back to Bloomington and get your degree. Disney will always be here."

Stunned and humbled, I walked out of his office with tears in my eyes. Talk about making a girl feel good. I truly had no idea that DJ and Manny were two of the best leaders I would ever have at Disney.

After returning to Bloomington, I got a call late one night from Jamie offering me the full-time position after graduation. When I returned after graduation, it was like I hadn't even left. So many of the amazing Cast Members were still at the Caribbean Beach Front Office. I was having the time of my life.

One of the beauties of working for a company as large as Disney is the ability to move roles and locations but still be employed by the same company. If I wanted to learn a new line of business, I could.

I was intrigued by two lines of business in particular - Disney Cruise Line and Disney Vacation Club.

After being at the Caribbean Beach Resort for 3 years, it was time to move on. Wanting to learn about DVC, I made a move to the first DVC property, Disney's Old Key West Resort. Disney Vacation Club is Disney's version of "timeshare". The beauty of the membership is you are staying in Disney's nicest, most luxurious resorts for the same cost of a "value" accommodation.

Being a Front Desk manager at Old Key West, I learned the ins and out of the membership. I thought to myself, 'I want to sell this. I want to help families become DVC Members.'

I knew not having sales experience would be an issue. I did a lot of soul-searching and goal setting. What was my ultimate goal? To become a DVC Guide.

I stayed part-time with DVC (at a DVC resort, of course!) and did pharmaceutical sales for two years. In the fall of 2004, I was on the Disney portal when I saw the posting for DVC Guides! I was over the moon excited and applied that second. A few weeks later, I had one interview that turned into a second interview on the spot. I was surprised since I had heard it typically took months to get through the process.

I was at home in Indiana for Christmas when my phone rang -

I was being offered the position of Vacation Club Guide! I was over the moon, excited, and a little shocked.

The first few years of being a Guide were amazing, and I loved it. I was awarded "Rookie of the Year" and hit the company's elite sales level called "Leadership Circle". My next goal was to be promoted to the "Cruise Team". This was a team of top performers who were selected to give presentations and sell onboard the Disney Cruise Line Fleet. In 2008, I was selected for the team.

Funny how the intrigue of my early 20's would be my life for nearly 12 years.

I loved traveling and making friends from around the world, as the crew on most cruise ships is not American. Working on a cruise ship is such a unique experience.

My life seemed perfect from the outside looking in. I was traveling the world and being paid handsomely to do so.

But I wasn't happy. I was literally living my dream and not happy. What was wrong with me?

I quickly realized that my life goals - what I really wanted - was a family. I loved being successful in my career. I loved winning sales awards and making a lot of money. But at the end of the day, I wasn't happy.

I remember shopping with my mom one day when the sales clerk learned I worked on ships. She went on and on....and on....about how jealous she was. I finally had to leave the store.

In summer 2017, I "swiped right" on a guy named Chris. 'He's a cutie,' I thought to myself. Coincidentally, he's from Indiana as well. Our first date was at my favorite sushi restaurant. We sat at the bar, talking, drinking, and eating until the restaurant closed. One of the things we chatted about were our goals. He was intrigued by what I did for a living. He'd been on two cruises and really liked them. I gave him a quick education on DVC. I shared that I wanted a family and wanted to start my own DVC resale company.

"What would that do for you"?

"Well, even though I wouldn't be working 'for' Disney anymore, I would still be working 'with' Disney. But this would allow me to fulfill my dream of traveling on my terms. I've wanted a lake house in Michigan near my family for the summers since I was 15," I said with a shy smile.

I'm normally 'too much' for most men. I make too much money. I have too many dreams. I'm too well-traveled for them. I was told at one point by a close male friend that I intimidate men, especially since I'd completed my first Ironman triathlon. I remember thinking, 'that's absurd, I'm

Unstoppable!

just me!'

As I was talking, I could see the wheels spinning in Chris's head. He had an extensive background in real estate. I didn't know it at the time, but he was incredibly entrepreneurial.

The end of the night came, and he asked if I would like to see him again.

"Yes! I leave for Europe tomorrow, but I'll be back in 3 weeks."

He thought I was brushing him off.

I most definitely was not.

I continued to sail around the world as the rest of my friends and family lived "normal" lives. They were all having babies, taking their firstborn to kindergarten, and spending their Saturday mornings at the little league park. I felt like an outsider looking in.

At work, crazy things started happening - I had sailed on the Christmas cruise for 8 years. I didn't mind since I didn't have a spouse and kids. The year my aunt passed away, I was told by one leader that he would happily find someone else to sail so I could spend time with my family. I was later pulled into another leader's office and given the third degree about it.

January 16, 2018, was my 20th anniversary with Walt Disney

World. I was so excited - most departments celebrate with a cake and balloons. Some will even have Mickey on hand for the celebration. Every Cast Member gets a shiny new 20-year pin for their name tag and a Simba statue. I wasn't scheduled on a cruise and was in the office that day. I figured this was by design. The day came and went - not a mention of my 20th. I wanted to see just how long it would take for someone to acknowledge my anniversary. After all, HR sends the statue and pin directly to my leader.

90 days. After 90 days, I finally went to my leader and asked for my pin and statue.

The next not-so-magical moment happened a few months later. I had approved vacation time for a month-long trip to Africa to run a marathon and climb Mount Kilimanjaro. Shortly after arriving in Nairobi, I got a text from my boss that I need to come back to take a three-night cruise. I wanted to climb through the phone. We were at a welcome dinner for the marathon we were running the next morning. My girlfriends could see I was visibly upset....I showed them the texts. They rolled their eyes and handed me a beer.

"You need a new job, my friend."

"How can they tell you to come do a three-night cruise? You're not in Miami - you're in Nairobi!"

The morning we left for Tanzania, I was on Facetime with Chris telling him what happened. He was just as stunned as I was. That week as we climbed Mount Kilimanjaro, I just kept asking God for a sign. What was I going to do? I knew I needed to make myself happy....DVC just wasn't it any more.

The bottom line is that I was scared. Scared to stay. Scared to make a move. I was scared.

When I returned from Africa, I continued to sail. DCL was going to a new destination – Bermuda, out of New York. My parents, sister, and brother in law joined me on the first of two back-to-back cruises. We kept joking they may be sailing without me if I get fired for taking approved vacation time. All joking aside, I was still incredibly upset about how the whole thing played out.

Meeting up with my family in New York and getting hugs from the 4 of them was exactly what I needed. The only person missing was Chris.

At the end of the two cruises, I was packing my suitcase to fly back to Orlando the next day. I had a habit of packing the night before to make debarkation easier the next morning. I always left my suitcase on the floor in front of the couch. I had done this over 400 times. Around 2am, I got up to use the restroom. On the way back to bed, I tripped over the suitcase and hit my face on the side bed panel. Disoriented, I realized I was covered in blood. I tried to get up but couldn't. A minute or so later, I was finally able to get up and turn on the lights......it looked like a crime scene. Not only was I covered in blood, but I later learned they had to steam clean the carpets and throw away the bedding.

I knew my nose was broken. When we returned to Orlando, I went straight from the airport to the 'Disney doctor'. Yup, sure enough - broken nose. I called one of the leaders at DVC to let them know since paperwork would be coming their way. I never got a call from a single leader to see how I was doing. It was as if it didn't even happen.

In the spring of 2019, I woke up one morning on the Disney Dream, looked in the mirror, and thought, I can't do this anymore. I knew this day would come. I knew I would wake up one day and think, today's the day. I called Chris - could I really quit my job? What the hell was I going to do for a living? He reminded me of our first date - my saying I wanted the flexibility to do what I want when I want. DVC resale, he said.

I hung up with him and picked the phone back up. It was time.

I gave a 4-week notice. I was scared out of my mind....this was the biggest leap of faith I had ever taken. The night I turned in my Disney ID, Chris and I went to dinner. We sat at the bar, and I remember having my very first panic attack. Working for Disney was a HUGE part of my identity.

After I was no longer in "Mickey's Navy" I spent a month in Indiana with my family. I traveled to the places I wanted to

Unstoppable!

travel.

I also set the groundwork for DVC Resale Experts.

Fast forward to January of 2023, and DVC Resale Experts now employs 5 people, not including me. The best part is that our team has the freedom to work from anywhere - we often joke about DVC PTSD, but honestly, we're not joking. Every single one of our team members has been asked to come back to work for DVC directly. Every single one said, 'no, thank you. I'm happy where I am.' We sold almost $10 million in 2022 and have huge goals for 2023.

Life is all about timing...you have to be ready to do something. But I will say this....don't wait too long.

Do it.

Do it, scared.

You have too much to lose....things you don't even know you have to lose. Life is so short. I am so thankful that I took the leap of faith and started this company. If I hadn't swiped right, if we had waited one more month, we wouldn't have our precious miracle baby (yes, I'm a Mom!!!). Had we waited one more day to inquire about our lake house in Michigan (yes, the lake house happened, too!) we may not have bought it.

I cherish my time with my family and friends, and I don't take a single day for granted.

About the Author

Theresa Seitz is an American-born entrepreneur.

She had a 24-year career with the Walt Disney Company before starting her own company in 2020. Theresa lives in Orlando, Florida, with her husband, son, and their Goldendoodle.

She gave birth to a miracle IVF baby six weeks before her 44th birthday.

An avid triathlete, Theresa has completed three full Ironman triathlons.

Theresa is passionate about spending time with family, sports, and travel. She is in the process of running a marathon on all seven continents.

Facebook: www.facebook.com/theresaseitz
Instagram: www.instagram.com/authentically.theresa

Valerie Thurman

From Frozen to failing forward

It was springtime, and money was tight.

I knew that I didn't want to have to work 2 or 3 jobs to make ends meet and able to do the extra things for my daughters. I had just completed the holiday season, where I not only had my full-time job, but I also worked two part-time jobs as well. While it did help with the bills and to provide a good Christmas for my family, I also missed out on dinners and special times with my daughters.

Online I saw different network marketing companies that talked about making money. I looked into two different ones but was still deciding. I didn't want to jump into something without really looking into it and having that "warm fuzzy feeling" about it.

Fast forward about six months, and it was the holiday season, but I was in a different job and didn't have to worry as much about bringing in extra money. However, I was still interesting in doing something more than my "day job." I had found myself exploring more items in the makeup area of life than I had in the past. There was one "magic" mascara that my daughters kept telling me about. I finally gave it a try and LOVED it. But this was during the busy nonstop time of my work season, so I told myself after the new year, I would look into it.

After the new year started, I explored two different companies. One was about health and wellness, and the other was makeup. After doing some research and having a friend's opinion, I decided on the company.

I joined and was excited about it and did what I saw others doing..... posting on social media about the great items. I was so excited to have the orders coming in from friends that were checking things out.

Shortly after starting the new journey, I met a friend out for a movie and some girl time. It took me completely by suprise when she asked me about what I was doing, how I liked it and wanted to join me! At this time, I didn't realize the importance of building a team or what to do next. Together we did the things we saw others doing, and we were following different top leaders in the company, comparing notes and cheering each other on!

Although I got "the looks" from my family, I was still excited about this new journey. Especially as I was able to use this new income to pay a monthly payment on a bill or be able to afford pizza and Redbox for the weekend. I was having fun posting the new monthly specials and talking to people about what I thought of the new products I was having fun trying.

This first year was fun, however, I also didn't know what I didn't know. I tried to learn the things but didn't understand the importance of building a team. After the "looks" from family, I was afraid to approach friends. Sure, I'd make the famous 100's list of those you thought would be good at this, but I didn't do anything with it. It was years later that I found out a couple friends were "interested" in joining me on this fun journey, but I never asked or started a conversation about it with them.

It was pretty exciting to share online about "my why" and the things this fun new opportunity paid for - like helping to pay for college books & other items needed for one daughter, helped with the purchase of a crib/changing table for my other daughter, and treating my mom to Red Lobster without worrying about the cost. These things felt good!

While I did the things the first year, there were so many things that also got in my way. Things like fear of what others would think, learning more about how I could succeed in this newfound adventure, and growing myself. Again, you don't know what you don't know.

During this first and second year, I'd sign up for the five-day courses or purchase the ones that would be $19.99 (or somewhere in that area). I'd watch, do the things that I felt were relevant, skip the things I didn't want to do, and try to continue doing the things the leaders in my company were saying to do. Some months would be great, and some months I'd get in my own way.

Fast forward to 2017.......it was the new year, and I was determined! I was still enrolling in courses but was looking at other ones, like one offered by Jim Rohn. I knew what I was doing wasn't working, so I knew I needed to do something different. As I was working to plan ahead, schedule things out, and be more intentional with my business, life happened.

My mom passed away somewhat unexpectedly, and it seemed inappropriate to be posting about makeup. So I stopped. I had talked with a dear friend about this, and she said I should continue on despite. I wished I had listened to her, but again I was too afraid of what others would think. This would be only the beginning of several years of my starting and stopping working my business.

Things in life continued on....working my day job, family life, my brother moving in with me, my daughters' lives continuing on the way that life does. I continued to do the challenges my uplines would put forth. Luckily I also had several loyal customers that would reach out when their products needed a refill. I was going on, but there was a lot to try to fit into each of my days this first year after the passing of my mom.

As the new year of 2018 started, I was finally getting into a rhythm of day-to-day life. Just as I finally felt like things were going to be okay, my brother unexpectedly passed away. This is the one thing that I took the hardest. Instead of being put into the fight or flight mode, I was in freeze mode. I couldn't move. I couldn't make decisions. I couldn't function. Being in this frozen, broken state, it not only affected my physically and emotionally but my health as well. I still had my online business, but it was hanging on by a thread.

This was also the first year that I went to my company Convention. They say convention changes things, and this was certainly true! I met Hope, whom I roomed with and had there for support. As an introvert and still struggling, Hope was a bit of a savior as she helped me get thru a rough day and helped make that first convention life-changing.

After I got back, I knew that I needed to move forward. I wanted to have more experiences like the one I just had. More friendships. More trips. To change lives of others, just like the stories that were shared during those days that were such a whirlwind but also life-changing.

I started to follow others that were outside of my company and enroll in monthly trainings so that I could learn more and make changes. I started reading books that would be mentioned in trainings or talked about by those in my company. However, I would still pick and choose which daily items to complete. Same in 30-day challenges - I would do the ones that seemed important or that sounded like fun. However, there were still those "ones" that I would roll my eyes at and skip altogether.

In 2019, I attended my second convention and met more lifelong friends. It was great meeting those that were on my team, along with others that were sideline sisters. This year Tara and Jessie were new roommates helped make amazing memories at convention.

To this day, Hope and Tara have played a huge part of keeping me on track and full of inspiration. It is crazy the friendships that can be made through this opportunity. We are there for each other in all areas of life. For family, thru tragedy, uncertainty, for support, and to cheer each other on! Life would be so different without not only their friendship but others that are on my team and those that I have met along this journey. These friendships are priceless.

Over the next couple of years, I continued on with learning from others, enrolling in 5-day programs, and the continuous start and stopping of my business. I couldn't get back into a good rhythm to continue each day, day in and day out. Some months would be really good, and some months I barely did much for my business.

I started to hear things like if you want your business to pay you like a business, then you need to treat it like a business. I knew that I wanted to be able to help others to generate an income thru this amazing opportunity and be able to have this as my "full-time job." I knew it was time to make that radical change.

It was the end of the summer 2021. School was starting again for my grandson. Fall was just around the corner. And I knew I wanted things to change. I wanted out of my "day" job so I would have more time freedom for my family, for my grandbabies, for myself.

I signed up for a five-day challenge in a new group run by a gal I had yet to follow. I had watched a quick daily training here or there that had her, but nothing too big. Somehow she spoke to me. She said things that I needed to hear. I knew I needed to follow her and hear more of her trainings.

She spoke of her one on one coaching. This SCARED me. I had done some training before, but I needed to truly invest in myself in this way. The thought of investing in one on one coaching not only scared me but it also made me curious. Is THIS what I've been missing and needing to advance me further? We had a meeting, and the thought of investing in myself, of having a coach that would be there for me specifically (not just a five-day course with a Q & A session at the end), scared and excited me. I KNEW this is what I needed.

This is what would help me get to where I wanted to go. So I made the jump!

The first call really showed my uncertainty and lack of confidence in myself. At times, I looked at myself in the mirror and wondered where my confidence went. Where was that gal that would make bold moves for the leadership position she wanted? I knew that there was going to be lots of hard work to be done to get back to where I once was and then to push forward to where I wanted to go.

The first couple of months, I was afraid to do even the most simplest of things for fear of doing it wrong. I was afraid. Afraid to fail. Here I was, taking that "big" leap that you hear others talk about - you know, that thing that propelled them forward in their dreams. I was secretly afraid of if I fail? Now that I've taken this big leap, invested in myself - that ride or die moment - and I was back frozen. Afraid to take action. Afraid to succeed. Afraid to fail. Afraid to make a decision. Afraid to move.

As the year 2022 started, I knew I had to do things differently. As this new year started, there were new systems that were introduced. As a "planner" type of personality, I liked systems. Notebooks and items to complete were my thing! So I got pretty colored pens that felt great to write with, set a January goal, and was determined I needed to treat my business as a business, not an expensive hobby. I was excited about the new systems as they spoke to me, and I focused on my first goal! January 2022 was great as I ended the month completing my first goal! I think that gave me the confidence I needed.

The new systems that were put into place at the beginning of the year helped me realize that I needed to work on my mindset. Although I have a background in meditation, and Reiki and a believer in energy healing, I hadn't used this in my day-to-day life for the last couple of years. This year, each day started with some meditation time. I am a believer in manifestation in energy work, and it felt good to start each day with guided meditation and affirmations.

The following months I was still doing the things that I thought were relevant and skipping the items that I didn't think were truly needed or that I didn't want to do. This time period also included a lot of start and stop, but I was growing. Every time I stopped, the next day would be Day 1 again of starting over. I would continue to let "life" or being frozen get in my way. But I was also working on personal development, growing my mindset, improving myself, doing the inner work.

As the year continued to go on, I knew that I was learning and growing. I could see the change, as could my coach. I knew that I needed to continue on this path of learning and implementing in order to grow not only my personal self but all areas that would allow my self-confidence to shine through.

This year I would continue to be in the top 10 of my team's monthly reports the majority of the time. I would earn "Baller Calls" and other incentives that were available the majority of the time. I would continue to do the inner work to increase my streaks of the days I did the things and less of the starting and stopping. I made some big goals for November, not only wrote down the things I wanted to achieve but said them out loud! My November of 2022, I landed in the top 3 of my team's reports, and it was one of the biggest month's in a very long time. I was so excited! I could see things starting to shift, starting to change.

As 2022 was winding down and the planning for 2023 was starting, I noticed my mindset was making some big changes. If I wanted the success that others had achieved, I needed to do the things that they did. No more skipping the stuff I thought was irrelevant or that I didn't want to do. I needed to commit to doing ALL the things. I needed to get good at doing the mundane things. Get good at the daily items, regardless of life, regardless if you feel like doing them. I needed to show up every day to back myself - to do the things I said I was going to do. Over the last year, I noticed that how I showed up in one area of my life is how I'd show up in all areas of my life. Either I'd get nothing done, or I'd be crazy productive and get everything done!

As 2023 started, I decided it was time to start backing myself and showing up as my next-level self in all areas of my life. Every year as you set your goals for your year, you should set one 30-day goal to be completed by the end of January. I am one of "those" people who have multiple alarms for my morning. Several to get out of bed, and then just alarms to make sure I check the time as I get ready for work. I decided that my January goal would be I would get out of bed on my first alarm. The first couple of days were hard, but as I would reach out to snooze it, I would tell myself that I will back myself and do what I said I was going to do. Words cannot describe how great it feels to get up on the first alarm and start your day on time. I am currently on track to meet that goal.

Having 2022 be the year of mindset growth, I am excited for 2023 to be the year of discipline. I am starting the year off being disciplined, starting my day when I say I am going to, and being disciplined in taking action. Each day is an improvement over the last. I am excited to see where 2023 takes me.

If you are wanting to get away from living paycheck to paycheck or working more than one job like I did....and not seeing your family, I understand. I get it.

This may be your sign that you need to consider an alternate stream of income. Maybe it's time to plan for your future. If this is you, here are four tips I can share with you so you can start making informed decisions:

1. Find something that speaks to you and jump in with both feet. Don't put off starting trying to find the "right" thing or the right time. Just start!

2. Personal Development and Mindset is HUGE! So pour into yourself and always be learning and growing.

3. Ask questions and lots of them. Even if the question is what is the most important item(s) that I should focus on first. You don't know what you don't know. So ask the questions.

4. Have FUN! Its crazy the things that happen when you are having fun as you learn and grow.

About the Author

Valerie Thurman is a mom, sister, Nan, and friend.

She has been with her network marketing company since 2015, hit several milestones, and showed others how they can also earn money from their phone.

When she isn't helping others feel confident in their own skin, Valerie likes to spend time with her family, having adventures with her grandchildren, and making memories.

She also enjoys practicing Reiki Healing.

Email: val.thurman@gmail.com
Facebook: www.facebook.com/valerie.thurman.33
Website: www.createyourselfbyvalerie.com

www.ingramcontent.com/pod-product-compliance
Lightning Source LLC
Chambersburg PA
CBHW051417290426
44109CB00016B/1336